Celebrate
The
Holidays

CRESCENT BOOKS

This edition is an enlarged version of the **BEST RECIPES CELEBRATE THE HOLIDAYS** cookbook.

©**1990, 1991 Campbell Soup Company**
"Campbell's", "Campbell's Fresh", "Franco-American" and "Swanson" are registered trademarks of Campbell Soup Company. "Vlasic" is a registered trademark of Vlasic Foods, Inc. "Mrs. Paul's" is a registered trademark of Mrs. Paul's Kitchens, Inc.

This edition was produced by the Publications Center in coordination with the Creative Food Center and Communications Center, Campbell Soup Company, Campbell Place, Camden, NJ 08103-1799.

Managing Editor: Pat Teberg
Contributing Editors: Julia Malloy, Flora Szatkowski
Home Economists: Lisa Miller, Patricia Owens, Margaret Romano
Food Stylist: Patricia A. Ward
Photographers: William R. Houssell, Robert Fazio, Nancy Principato, Maggie Wochele
Art Director: Lee Singer
Accessories Stylists: Lee Wilson, Lynn Wilson

Pictured on the front cover: Herb Cheesecake (*see recipe, page* 12), Broiled Shrimp Dijon (*see recipe, page* 15), Hot and Spicy Chicken Wings (*see recipe, page* 11) and Tomato-Olive Salsa (*see recipe, page* 19)

Pictured on the back cover: Fresh Vegetable Marinade (*see recipe, page* 8), Herb-Stuffed Turkey (*see recipe, page* 30) and Christmas Stollen (*see recipe, page* 88)

ISBN: 0-517-05244-X

Library of Congress Catalog Card Number: 91-61029

This edition was published by:
Crescent Books
Distributed by Outlet Book Company
A Random House Company
225 Park Avenue South
New York, New York 10003

Printed and bound in Yugoslavia

9 8 7 6 5 4 3 2 1

Microwave cooking times in this book are approximate. These recipes have been tested in 650- to 700-watt microwave ovens. Foods cooked in lower-wattage ovens may require longer cooking times. Use the cooking times as guidelines and check for doneness before adding more time.

Celebrate
The
Holidays

Introduction   4

Party Snacks and Appetizers   6

Entrées for Entertaining   20

Holiday Planned-Overs   38

Holiday Breakfasts and Brunches   48

Bowl-Time Soups and Sandwiches   60

Special Side Dishes   70

Festive Desserts   86

Index   94

The joyous spirit of the season radiates from the home, where family and friends gather for fun and food. Campbell Soup Company wants to be a part of your festivities with *Celebrate The Holidays*. This colorful holiday cookbook offers fabulous foods made easy using top-quality convenience foods such as "Campbell's" soups, "Campbell's Fresh" vegetables, "Franco-American" gravy, "Mrs. Paul's" frozen foods, "Swanson" broths and "Vlasic" olives.

Beginning with the Thanksgiving feast and ending with football in January, the holidays are the perfect time for getting together with family and friends. Neighborhood caroling. New Year's parties. An intimate dinner for two. Large family get-togethers. Football bowl games. Christmas-time brunch. All these special occasions call for extra-special foods.

In *Celebrate The Holidays*, you'll find fabulous recipes for all kinds of holiday parties. There's a traditional roast turkey with stuffing and a boneless veal shoulder stuffed with pesto; picture-perfect mushroom pastries and easy, microwavable dips for chips and vegetables; Italian-style pizzas and Southwestern chili. You'll also discover soups and side dishes to set off your entrées, breakfast and brunch specialties, as well as delightful desserts.

Included, too, are valuable hints to make your party a success. Along with time-saving microwave directions for many recipes, read the many make-ahead tips and serving suggestions. As you turn the pages of this cookbook, you'll find inspiration for some great entertaining and, perhaps, create new holiday traditions for your family.

Holiday Helpers

You can count on experienced kitchen help when you rely on the Campbell family of quality products. Your grandparents depended on Campbell's tasty, convenient-to-use products to plan their holiday festivities, and now you'll find exciting new recipes in this cookbook that reflect today's tastes.

"Swanson" ready to serve chicken and beef broths are real time-savers. They provide long-simmered, full flavor in the time it takes to open a can. It's that easy! Use them in sauces, soups, salad dressings, stuffings and side dishes. If you prefer foods with reduced sodium, substitute "Swanson" "Natural Goodness" chicken broth with ⅓ less salt than regular "Swanson" broth.

"Franco-American" gravy is great to use if you've never mastered gravy making or want to avoid the hassle. But even the most competent cook finds the rich, full flavor of "Franco-American" gravy works wonders in hearty sandwiches, tasty appetizers, side dishes and a wide range of main dishes, from omelets to roast beef.

Begin a delicious casserole or entrée with "Campbell's" condensed soups, available in several varieties from all-time favorite tomato and cream of mushroom to contemporary nacho cheese and cream of broccoli. Generations have used these soups to season stews and meat loaves and to freshen the flavor of leftovers, and this cookbook will show you more creative and delicious ways to cook with soup that Grandma never taught you. Use them in every part of your meal: soups, salads, appetizers, side dishes and even desserts!

And, don't forget to include an assortment of "Vlasic" olives, capers and maraschino cherries in your holiday festivities. These shimmering jewels add color and excitement to relish trays and a multitude of recipes. Olives and capers impart sophisticated flavors to many appetizers, salads and main dishes while ruby-red maraschino cherries star in many holiday breads and desserts.

In your grocery store's produce section, look for "Campbell's Fresh" vegetables: fresh, all natural mushrooms; hydroponically-grown butterhead lettuce and flavorful, vine-ripened tomatoes. You'll enjoy these high-quality fresh vegetables in salads and sandwiches, but you also can include the regular and exotic mushroom varieties in appetizers, soups and entrées of all kinds.

Campbell Soup Company wishes you and yours a joyous holiday season filled with good friends and good food, and all the best in the coming new year.

Party Snacks and Appetizers

Whether you're cooking up a cocktail party for dozens or preparing an intimate New Year's celebration for two, the foods you serve set the mood. Choose from easy-to-prepare dips for vegetables and chips, spectacular spreads, hot and spicy meatballs, marinated vegetables and an exciting array of savory pastries and finger foods. Combining two or three of these appetizers will make any occasion even more special.

Crab with Caper-Dill Dip

Crab with Caper-Dill Dip

Dip deviled crab miniatures, fried shrimp and fresh vegetables in the tangy dip for a zesty snack. Pictured opposite.

2 packages (7 ounces *each*) Mrs. Paul's frozen deviled crab miniatures, fried shrimp or scallops
½ cup mayonnaise
1 tablespoon chopped Vlasic capers
1 teaspoon chopped fresh dill or ¼ teaspoon dried dill weed, crushed
1 teaspoon lemon juice
Vlasic capers and chopped fresh dill for garnish

1. To make dip: Remove sauce packet from crab miniature box. Return crab to freezer until ready to heat. In small bowl, combine sauce packet contents, mayonnaise, capers, dill and lemon juice. Cover; refrigerate until serving time, at least 2 hours.

2. Prepare crab according to package directions. Serve with dip. Garnish dip with capers and fresh dill, if desired. Makes about 26 appetizers.

Fresh Vegetable Marinade

This colorful appetizer will add pizzazz at a cocktail party. Serve with decorative toothpicks. Pictured opposite and on back cover.

1 cup vegetable or olive oil
½ cup vinegar
1 clove garlic, minced
1 teaspoon dried oregano leaves, crushed
¼ teaspoon pepper

2 packages (8 ounces *each*) Campbell's Fresh mushrooms
2 cups broccoli flowerets
2 cups cauliflowerets
2 cups sweet red pepper cut into 1-inch squares
2 cups diagonally sliced carrots

1. In large bowl, combine oil, vinegar, garlic, oregano and pepper. Add mushrooms, broccoli, cauliflower, red pepper and carrots; toss to coat.

2. Cover; refrigerate until serving time, at least 4 hours, stirring occasionally. Makes 12 cups or 16 appetizer servings.

Olive Medley Mediterranean

This easy-to-make relish adds lots of flavor to main dishes and sandwiches. Pictured on page 67.

1 can (6 ounces) Vlasic pitted ripe olives, drained
1 jar (5 ounces) Vlasic pimento-stuffed Spanish olives, drained
½ cup drained Vlasic cocktail onions

2 tablespoons olive oil
2 tablespoons red wine vinegar
3 cloves garlic, minced
½ teaspoon crushed red pepper
½ teaspoon ground allspice
¼ teaspoon dried oregano leaves, crushed

1. In large glass bowl, combine all ingredients; toss to mix well. Cover; refrigerate until serving time, at least 4 hours, stirring occasionally.

2. Serve chilled or at room temperature with decorative toothpicks. Makes 3 cups or 12 appetizer servings.

Fresh Vegetable Marinade

Spicy Meatballs

No ordinary meatballs here — these meatballs get their added zip from sausage, green chilies and chili powder.

1 pound ground beef
¼ pound bulk pork sausage
½ cup chopped onion
¼ cup fine dry bread crumbs
1 can (4 ounces) chopped green
   chilies

2 tablespoons chopped fresh
   parsley
2 eggs, beaten
1 teaspoon chili powder
2 cloves garlic, minced
1 can (10½ ounces) Franco-
   American golden pork gravy

1. Preheat oven to 425°F. In medium bowl, thoroughly mix beef, sausage, onion, crumbs, chilies, parsley, eggs, chili powder and garlic. Shape into 1-inch meatballs. Place on rack in broiler pan. Bake 25 minutes or until browned.

2. Place meatballs in 10-inch skillet. Add gravy. Over medium heat, heat through, stirring occasionally. Pour into serving bowl; serve with decorative toothpicks. Makes about 40 appetizers.

Gingered Turkey Meatballs

Party-goers will love the Oriental flavors that season these tasty morsels.

1 pound ground raw turkey
½ cup gingersnap crumbs
¼ cup finely chopped onion
2 tablespoons soy sauce, divided
½ teaspoon curry powder
⅛ teaspoon pepper

2 tablespoons vegetable oil
1 can (10½ ounces) Franco-
   American chicken gravy
1 tablespoon brown sugar
½ teaspoon grated fresh ginger

1. In medium bowl, thoroughly mix turkey, gingersnap crumbs, onion, *1 tablespoon* of the soy sauce, the curry and pepper. Shape into 1-inch meatballs.

2. In 10-inch skillet over medium heat, in hot oil, cook meatballs, a few at a time, until browned on all sides. Remove meatballs as they brown. Spoon off fat. Return all meatballs to skillet.

3. Stir in gravy, sugar, ginger and remaining soy sauce. Heat to boiling. Reduce heat to low. Cover; simmer 20 minutes or until meatballs are done, stirring occasionally. Pour into serving bowl; serve with decorative toothpicks. Makes about 34 appetizers.

Hot and Spicy Chicken Wings

You can adjust the heat in these appetizers by changing the amount of hot pepper sauce. Pictured on front cover.

20 chicken wings (about 3 pounds)
2 tablespoons vegetable oil
1 can (10½ ounces) Franco-American brown gravy with onions
¼ cup ketchup
1½ teaspoons hot pepper sauce
1 teaspoon brown sugar
½ teaspoon vinegar

1. Cut tips off chicken wings; discard tips or save for another use. Cut wings at joints to form 40 pieces; brush with oil.

2. To make sauce: In small bowl, combine gravy, ketchup, hot pepper sauce, sugar and vinegar; set aside.

3. Arrange chicken wings on rack in broiler pan. Broil, 6 inches from heat, 40 minutes, turning and brushing with sauce during last 15 minutes of broiling. Makes 40 appetizers.

Lime-Ginger Skewered Chicken

1 can (14½ ounces) Swanson clear ready to serve chicken broth
2 tablespoons lime juice
2 tablespoons vegetable oil
2 tablespoons soy sauce
1 tablespoon brown sugar
¼ teaspoon ground ginger
¼ teaspoon crushed red pepper
2 cloves garlic, minced
2 pounds boneless, skinless chicken breasts, cut into 1-inch pieces
2 tablespoons cornstarch

1. To make marinade: In 13- by 9-inch baking dish, combine broth, lime juice, oil, soy sauce, sugar, ginger, crushed red pepper and garlic.

2. On 6 skewers, thread about 5 pieces of the chicken. Arrange in baking dish, turning to coat with marinade. Cover; refrigerate 1 hour.

3. Arrange kabobs on rack in broiler pan, reserving marinade. In 1-quart saucepan, stir marinade into cornstarch. Over medium heat, cook until sauce boils and thickens, stirring constantly. Remove from heat.

4. Broil chicken, 4 inches from heat, 10 to 12 minutes or until chicken is no longer pink, turning and brushing often with sauce. Heat remaining sauce through; serve with kabobs. Makes 6 kabobs.

TIP: If using wooden skewers, soak in water 30 minutes before using.

Herb Cheesecake

When you're expecting a crowd, this creamy cheesecake is a delicious choice for the buffet table. Pictured opposite and on front cover.

3 packages (8 ounces *each*)
  cream cheese, softened
2 cups sour cream, divided
1 can (10¾ ounces) Campbell's
  condensed cream of celery
  or cream of asparagus soup
3 eggs
½ cup grated Romano or Asiago
  cheese
2 cloves garlic, minced
1 tablespoon cornstarch
2 tablespoons finely chopped
  fresh basil leaves or
  2 teaspoons dried basil
  leaves, crushed

1 tablespoon finely chopped
  thyme leaves or 1 teaspoon
  dried thyme leaves, crushed
1 teaspoon finely chopped fresh
  tarragon leaves or
  ¼ teaspoon dried tarragon
  leaves, crushed
½ teaspoon cracked pepper
  Sweet red pepper strips, lemon
  peel twists and assorted
  fresh herbs for garnish
  Crackers, melba toast or fresh
  cut-up vegetables

1. Preheat oven to 350°F. Grease side and bottom of 9-inch springform pan.

2. In covered food processor* or large mixer bowl, combine cream cheese, *1 cup* of the sour cream and the soup. Blend in food processor or beat with mixer at medium speed until smooth. Add eggs, Romano cheese, garlic, cornstarch, basil, thyme, tarragon and pepper. Blend or beat until smooth. Turn into prepared springform pan; place on jelly-roll pan.

3. Bake 1 hour or until light brown (top may crack). Turn off oven; let stand in oven 30 minutes more. Cool in pan on wire rack. Cover; refrigerate until serving time, at least 4 hours or overnight.

4. Spread remaining sour cream over cheesecake. Garnish with red pepper strips, lemon peel twists and fresh herbs, if desired. Serve with crackers. Makes 16 appetizer servings.

*Quantity of mixture requires an 8-cup capacity food processor.

Herb Cheesecake

Crab Parmesan Toasts

Thin slices of French bread can be used instead of English Muffins. Just toast before topping with the savory crab mixture.

1 can (10¾ ounces) Campbell's condensed cream of mushroom soup
1 pound (about 3 cups) lump crabmeat, flaked
½ cup chopped celery
¼ cup sliced green onions

¼ teaspoon grated lemon peel
1 tablespoon lemon juice
8 English muffins, split, toasted and cut in half
½ cup grated Parmesan cheese
Paprika

1. In medium bowl, stir together soup, crabmeat, celery, onions, lemon peel and lemon juice. Spread about *1½ tablespoons* of the crab mixture on each muffin piece.

2. Arrange on 2 baking sheets; sprinkle with Parmesan and paprika.

3. Broil, 4 inches from heat, 5 minutes or until lightly browned. Serve immediately. Makes 32 appetizers.

Nachos Olé!

For halftime fare during the next holiday game or as a midnight nibble to ring in the new year, you can prepare this fast-fixing snack in the middle of the party without leaving your guests for more than a few minutes.

4 cups tortilla chips
1 can (11 ounces) Campbell's condensed nacho cheese soup/dip
¼ cup milk

Sliced Vlasic pitted ripe olives, chopped sweet red pepper and sliced green onions for garnish

1. Arrange chips on cookie sheet. Bake at 400°F. for 5 minutes or until warm. Meanwhile, in 1-quart saucepan, stir soup until smooth. Stir in milk until blended. Over medium heat, heat until warm, stirring often.

2. Arrange warm chips on serving platter. Drizzle soup mixture over chips. Garnish with olives, pepper and green onions, if desired. Makes 1½ cups sauce or 8 appetizer servings.

TO MICROWAVE: In 4-cup glass measure or 1-quart microwave-safe casserole, stir soup until smooth. Stir in milk until blended. Cover with vented plastic wrap or lid; microwave on HIGH 3 minutes or until hot and bubbling, stirring twice during heating. Arrange chips in single layer on 2 microwave-safe serving platters. Microwave 1 platter, uncovered, on HIGH 1 minute or until chips are warm, rotating plate once during cooking. Drizzle *half* of the soup mixture over chips. Garnish with olives, pepper and green onions, if desired. Repeat with remaining chips, soup mixture and garnish.

Broiled Shrimp Dijon

For a change of pace, broil fresh shrimp with a spicy barbecue sauce the next time you want to serve shrimp cocktail. Pictured on front cover.

1 can (10¾ ounces) Campbell's
    condensed tomato soup
1 clove garlic, minced
2 tablespoons vegetable oil
1 tablespoon brown sugar
1 tablespoon Dijon-style mustard
1 teaspoon lemon juice
½ teaspoon hot pepper sauce
1 pound extra-large shrimp
    (about 24)

1. To make marinade: In 2-quart saucepan, stir together soup, garlic, oil, sugar, mustard, lemon juice and hot pepper sauce. Over medium heat, cook until mixture boils and sugar is dissolved, stirring occasionally. Remove from heat.

2. Shell and devein shrimp, leaving tails intact. Place in large bowl; add marinade. Cover; refrigerate 2 hours.

3. Remove shrimp from bowl, reserving marinade. Arrange shrimp on rack in broiler pan. Broil, 4 inches from heat, 8 minutes or until shrimp are pink, turning once and brushing often with marinade.

4. Meanwhile, in 1-quart saucepan over medium heat, heat remaining marinade to boiling, stirring often. Serve with shrimp. Makes about 24 appetizers.

Stuffed Mushrooms Florentine

4 packages (8 ounces *each*)
    Campbell's Fresh
    mushrooms (about 70)
4 tablespoons butter or
    margarine, divided
½ cup finely chopped onion
¼ cup finely chopped walnuts
2 cloves garlic, minced
1 package (10 ounces) frozen
    chopped spinach, thawed
    and well drained
½ cup grated Parmesan cheese
1 tablespoon chopped fresh dill
    or 1 teaspoon dried dill
    weed, crushed
⅛ teaspoon pepper
½ teaspoon salt

1. Remove stems from mushrooms; chop enough stems to equal *1 cup*. Set aside. Preheat oven to 400°F.

2. In 3-quart saucepan over medium heat, in *2 tablespoons* hot butter, cook onion, walnuts and garlic 3 minutes, stirring occasionally. Add chopped mushroom stems and spinach. Cook 5 minutes or until liquid is evaporated, stirring occasionally. Remove from heat. Stir in Parmesan, dill and pepper.

3. Melt remaining butter. Lightly brush mushroom caps with melted butter; sprinkle with salt. Fill caps with spinach mixture. Arrange *half* of the filled mushroom caps on rack in broiler pan. Bake 15 minutes or until mushrooms are tender. Bake remaining mushrooms. Makes about 70 appetizers.

Mushroom Crescents

Each bite of these flaky pastries is packed with luscious mushroom flavor. Pictured opposite.

1 package (3 ounces) cream
   cheese, softened
½ cup butter or margarine,
   softened
1 cup all-purpose flour
⅛ teaspoon salt
2 tablespoons butter or margarine
2 packages (8 ounces *each*)
   Campbell's Fresh mushrooms,
   finely chopped (about 5 cups)

¼ cup finely chopped onion or
   shallots
2 tablespoons dry sherry
¼ teaspoon salt
   Dash pepper
1 egg, slightly beaten
   Grated Parmesan cheese

1. To make pastry: In medium bowl, beat together cream cheese and ½ cup butter. Add flour and ⅛ teaspoon salt, stirring until well blended. Shape into ball; wrap in plastic wrap. Refrigerate until firm but not hard, about 40 minutes.

2. To make mushroom filling: In 10-inch skillet over medium heat, in 2 tablespoons hot butter, cook mushrooms and onion until tender and liquid is evaporated, stirring occasionally. Stir in sherry, ¼ teaspoon salt and the pepper; remove from heat and cool.

3. Preheat oven to 375°F. On well floured surface, roll *half* of the pastry to ⅛-inch thickness. Using 3-inch round cutter, cut into 12 rounds.

4. Spoon about *2 teaspoons* mushroom filling in center of each round. Fold pastry over to make crescent shape; seal edges together by pressing with tines of fork.

5. Repeat with remaining pastry and filling.

6. Arrange on baking sheet. Brush with egg; sprinkle with Parmesan. Bake 20 minutes or until golden brown. Serve warm or at room temperature. Makes 24 appetizers.

TIP: To make mushroom-shaped pastries shown in photo, prepare an additional ½ recipe of pastry. Roll to ¼-inch thickness; cut into twenty-four 2-inch triangles. To make each mushroom-shaped pastry: Use one crescent pastry for top of mushroom. Place a point of one triangle in center of each crescent on straight edge. Using fingers, gently press point of triangle into crescent to seal. With spatula, transfer to baking sheet. Brush with beaten egg; sprinkle with Parmesan. Bake as directed in step 6.

Mushroom Crescents

Feta-Olive Turnovers

Frozen puff pastry makes these tasty triangles a cinch to assemble. Double the recipe if you're expecting a crowd.

1 sheet (from 17¼-ounce package) frozen ready to bake puff pastry sheets
1 egg
1 teaspoon water
1 package (3 ounces) cream cheese, softened
1 tablespoon Vlasic ripe olive liquid

¼ cup sliced Vlasic pitted ripe olives
¼ cup crumbled feta cheese
2 tablespoons diced pimento
2 tablespoons chopped fresh parsley
¼ teaspoon dried oregano leaves, crushed
¼ teaspoon garlic powder

1. Thaw puff pastry sheet according to package directions. In small cup, stir together egg and water; set aside.

2. In small bowl, beat together cream cheese and olive liquid until smooth. Stir in sliced olives, feta cheese, pimento, parsley, oregano and garlic powder; set aside. Preheat oven to 400°F.

3. On lightly floured surface, roll pastry to 12- by 12-inch square; cut into sixteen 3-inch squares. Top each with some of the cream cheese mixture. Brush edges of pastry with egg mixture, fold in half to form triangles. Seal edges together by pressing with tines of fork. Transfer to baking sheet. Brush again with egg mixture.

4. Bake 12 to 15 minutes or until turnovers are golden. Makes 16 appetizers.

Olive-Stuffed Cheese Balls

Hide a succulent olive in the cheesy pastry for a tangy appetizer nibble. Choose green or ripe olives according to your taste.

1 cup packaged biscuit mix
1 cup shredded sharp Cheddar cheese (4 ounces)
3 tablespoons milk
2 tablespoons butter or margarine, melted

½ teaspoon dried thyme leaves, crushed
½ teaspoon dried oregano leaves, crushed
24 Vlasic pitted large ripe or pimento-stuffed Spanish olives, well drained

1. Preheat oven to 400°F. Grease cookie sheet.

2. To make pastry: In medium bowl, thoroughly combine biscuit mix, cheese, milk, butter, thyme and oregano. Using *1 rounded teaspoon* of the pastry for each, mold pastry around each olive.

3. Arrange 1 inch apart on prepared baking sheet. Bake 10 to 12 minutes or until lightly browned. Serve warm. Makes 24 appetizers.

Tomato-Olive Salsa

Add zesty Southwestern flavor and color to your table. For serving ideas, see photo on front cover.

3 cups chopped Campbell's Fresh tomatoes
¾ cup Vlasic pitted ripe olives cut lengthwise into slices
¼ cup sliced green onions
2 tablespoons lime juice
1 tablespoon seeded and chopped Vlasic hot jalapeno peppers

1 tablespoon chopped fresh cilantro
1 clove garlic, minced
Toasted French bread, pita, tortilla chips or fresh cut-up vegetables

In medium bowl, combine all ingredients; stir gently to mix. Cover; refrigerate until serving time, at least 2 hours. Serve with toasted French bread. Makes 3¾ cups.

Pecan-Olive Canapes

1 package (8 ounces) cream cheese, softened
½ cup Vlasic salad chunky style Spanish olives

½ cup pecan halves
¼ cup mayonnaise
10 slices whole wheat bread, crusts removed

1. In covered food processor, combine cheese, olives, pecans and mayonnaise. Blend just until olives and nuts are chopped.

2. Spread olive mixture on bread. Cut each slice into 4 pieces. Cover; refrigerate until serving time. Makes 40 appetizers.

Basil-Mushroom Dip

1 tablespoon vegetable oil
1 package (8 ounces) Campbell's Fresh mushrooms, finely chopped
½ teaspoon dried basil leaves, crushed

⅓ cup chopped green onions
1 cup sour cream
⅛ teaspoon salt
⅛ teaspoon pepper
Crackers or fresh cut-up vegetables

1. In 10-inch skillet over medium heat, in hot oil, cook mushrooms and basil about 5 minutes or until liquid is evaporated, stirring occasionally. Add green onions; cook 1 minute more. Remove from heat; cool slightly.

2. In medium bowl, stir together mushroom mixture, sour cream, salt and pepper. Cover; refrigerate until serving time, at least 2 hours. Serve with crackers. Makes 1½ cups.

Entrées for Entertaining

Here's a wide selection of roasts, chops and special one-dish meals to add a festive air to holiday entertaining. With a little planning and preparation, spectacular entrées, such as Pesto-Stuffed Veal Roast or Herb-Stuffed Turkey, make an ideal centerpiece for any special occasion. If you need a fast-cooking main course, Lemon Garlic Shrimp or crispy Fish with Caper Salsa are great choices. Flavorful sauces and gravies complete the chapter.

Ginger Beef Stir-Fry

Ginger Beef Stir-Fry

Shredded lettuce makes a crunchy base for this taste-of-the-Orient beef stir-fry. Pictured opposite.

- 1 pound boneless beef sirloin steak, cut ¾ inch thick
- 2 tablespoons cornstarch
- 1 can (14½ ounces) Swanson clear ready to serve beef broth, divided
- 3 tablespoons soy sauce
- 1 clove garlic, minced
- ½ teaspoon grated fresh ginger
- ¼ teaspoon crushed red pepper
- 3 tablespoons vegetable oil, divided
- 1 package (8 ounces) Campbell's Fresh mushrooms, sliced
- 2 cups broccoli flowerets
- 1 cup sweet red pepper strips
  Shredded lettuce, hot cooked rice or noodles

1. Freeze meat 1 hour to firm for easier slicing. Slice across the grain into very thin strips.

2. For marinade: In medium bowl, stir together cornstarch, *½ cup* of the broth, the soy sauce, garlic, ginger and crushed red pepper. Add beef; stir to coat. Let stand 30 minutes.

3. In 10-inch skillet or wok over high heat, in *1 tablespoon* hot oil, cook mushrooms and broccoli, stirring quickly and frequently (stir-frying) until tender-crisp. Add red pepper strips; cook 2 minutes more or until tender-crisp. Transfer to bowl.

4. In same skillet or wok over high heat, heat remaining oil until hot. Remove beef from marinade; discard marinade. Add beef; stir-fry just until color changes. Stir in mushroom mixture and the remaining broth. Cook until mixture boils and thickens, stirring constantly. Serve over lettuce. Makes 6 cups or 4 servings.

Roast Beef with Dijon Gravy

1 can (10½ ounces) Franco-American au jus gravy
2 tablespoons Dijon-style mustard
2 cloves garlic, minced
¼ teaspoon pepper

3- pound boneless beef sirloin tip roast
1 can (10¼ ounces) Franco-American beef gravy
Hot mashed potatoes

1. To make marinade: In 2-quart casserole, stir together au jus gravy, mustard, garlic and pepper. Pierce roast with skewer. Place in casserole, turning roast to coat. Cover; refrigerate at least 4 hours, turning roast occasionally.

2. Remove roast; reserve marinade. Place roast on rack in roasting pan. Insert meat thermometer into thickest part of roast. Roast at 325°F. for 1½ to 2 hours or until internal temperature is 160°F. for medium doneness. Remove roast to platter; keep warm. Let stand 10 minutes before carving.

3. Meanwhile, to make gravy, remove rack from roasting pan. Stir reserved marinade and the beef gravy into drippings in pan. Over medium heat, heat to boiling, stirring to loosen browned bits. Remove and discard strings from roast. Serve gravy with slices of roast beef and mashed potatoes. Makes 12 servings.

Beef Scallops in Burgundy Sauce

1- pound beef top round steak, cut ½ inch thick
2 tablespoons vegetable oil, divided
2 cups sliced Campbell's Fresh mushrooms
2 medium onions, sliced
2 cloves garlic, minced

⅓ cup Burgundy or other dry red wine
¼ teaspoon pepper
1 can (14½ ounces) Swanson clear ready to serve beef broth
2 tablespoons cornstarch
Hot cooked rice (optional)

1. Cut beef into 8 pieces, each about 2 inches square. Place each piece between plastic wrap; with meat mallet, pound to ⅛-inch thickness.

2. In 10-inch skillet over medium heat, in *1 tablespoon* hot oil, brown beef on both sides, a few at a time, adding more oil as necessary. Remove with fork to platter; set aside and keep warm.

3. Add remaining 1 tablespoon oil to drippings in skillet. Over medium heat, in hot drippings, cook mushrooms, onions and garlic 5 minutes or until onions are tender, stirring occasionally.

4. Add wine and pepper; cook until liquid is reduced by half. In 2-cup glass measure, stir broth into cornstarch. Stir into skillet; cook until mixture boils and thickens, stirring constantly. Return beef to skillet; heat through. Serve with rice, if desired. Makes 4 servings.

Pesto-Stuffed Veal Roast

Start with prepared pesto sauce to make this easy, yet elegant, stuffing.

½ cup prepared pesto sauce
1½ cups plain croutons
4- pound rolled boneless veal
    shoulder roast
    Pepper
8 slices bacon

1 can (14½ ounces) Swanson
    clear ready to serve
    chicken broth
2 tablespoons water
2 tablespoons cornstarch
    Hot cooked rice

1. In small bowl, stir together pesto sauce and croutons. Preheat oven to 425°F.

2. Untie roast and lay flat on plastic wrap. If roast is uneven in thickness, slice off thicker parts of veal and place along edges of roast to make uniform rectangle. Cover with plastic wrap. With meat mallet or rolling pin, pound to 1-inch thickness.

3. Sprinkle meat with pepper. Spread crouton mixture down center of roast. Fold sides over stuffing. Tie with kitchen string crosswise at 2-inch intervals, starting at center of roast. Lay bacon slices over roast, overlapping slightly. Place roast on rack in shallow roasting pan. Insert meat thermometer into thickest part of roast.

4. Roast, uncovered, 40 minutes or until bacon is crisp. Reduce heat to 325°F. Add broth to pan. Cover with foil. Roast 45 to 55 minutes more or until internal temperature of roast is 170°F. Remove roast to platter; keep warm. Let stand 10 minutes before carving.

5. Meanwhile, skim fat from drippings. In 2-quart saucepan, heat drippings to boiling. Over medium heat, boil, uncovered, 8 minutes or until drippings are reduced to 2 cups. In cup, stir water into cornstarch. Stir into drippings. Cook until mixture boils and thickens, stirring constantly.

6. Remove and discard strings from roast. Slice roast and serve with gravy and rice. Makes 10 servings.

Vegetable-Stuffed Flank Steak

For an elegant but simple accompaniment, serve with steamed acorn squash slices and asparagus spears. Pictured opposite.

4 tablespoons butter or margarine, divided	**1½ slices bread, cut into ½-inch cubes (1 cup)**
½ cup sliced green onions	**1 egg, beaten**
½ cup finely chopped celery	**⅛ teaspoon salt**
½ cup finely chopped carrot	**2 pounds beef flank steak**
½ teaspoon dried thyme leaves, crushed, divided	**1 can (14½ ounces) Swanson clear ready to serve beef broth, divided**
½ teaspoon rubbed sage, divided	**2 tablespoons cornstarch**

1. In 5-quart oven-safe Dutch oven over medium heat, in 2 *tablespoons* hot butter, cook onions, celery, carrot and ¼ *teaspoon each* of the thyme and sage until vegetables are almost tender, stirring often.

2. In medium bowl, combine bread cubes, egg, salt and cooked vegetable mixture; toss to mix.

3. Place steak between sheets of plastic wrap; with meat mallet or rolling pin, pound steak to ½-inch thickness. Rub steak with remaining thyme and sage.

4. Spread vegetable mixture evenly over steak to within 1 inch of edges. Roll up steak from long end, jelly-roll fashion. Tie with kitchen string crosswise at 2-inch intervals, starting at center of steak. Tie lengthwise, tucking ends of beef underneath.

5. In same Dutch oven over medium heat, in remaining butter, brown steak on all sides. Add *1 cup* of the broth; heat to boiling. Cover; bake at 350°F. for 1½ to 2 hours or until tender.

6. Transfer beef to platter; keep warm. Pour drippings into 4-cup glass measure; skim fat from drippings. Pour 1½ *cups* of the drippings through strainer back into Dutch oven.

7. In cup, stir remaining broth into cornstarch; gradually stir into drippings. Cook over medium heat until mixture boils and thickens, stirring constantly.

8. Remove and discard strings from beef. Slice and serve with gravy. Makes 8 servings.

Vegetable-Stuffed Flank Steak

Spiced Pork Loin with Sweet Potatoes

Use fresh Brussels sprouts when they're in season. Pictured opposite.

2 teaspoons dry mustard
¼ teaspoon pepper
3- pound boneless pork loin roast
15 whole cloves
2 tablespoon butter or margarine
2 medium onions, cut into small wedges
2 cloves garlic, minced

2 packages (12 ounces *each*) Mrs. Paul's frozen candied sweet potatoes
⅓ cup water
1 package (10 ounces) frozen Brussels sprouts
2 teaspoons lemon juice

1. In cup, combine mustard and pepper; rub over roast. Using skewer, pierce top of roast 15 times; insert whole cloves into holes.

2. In 5-quart oven-safe Dutch oven over medium heat, in hot butter, brown roast on all sides along with onions and garlic. Insert meat thermometer into thickest part of roast. Add sweet potatoes and water. Sprinkle candied sauce mix over potatoes. Heat to boiling.

3. Cover; bake at 325°F. for 55 minutes. Add Brussels sprouts. Cover; bake 40 minutes more or until internal temperature of roast reaches 170°F. and sprouts are tender.

4. Transfer roast and vegetables to platter. Strain drippings; add in lemon juice. Serve sauce with roast and vegetables. Makes 8 to 10 servings.

Piquant Pork Chops

2 tablespoons olive oil
6 boneless pork loin chops, each cut ½ inch thick (about 1 pound)
1 medium onion, finely chopped
½ teaspoon dried basil leaves, crushed
¼ teaspoon pepper

1 can (11 ounces) Campbell's condensed zesty tomato soup
½ cup water
1 medium orange, sliced
1 medium green pepper, cut into strips
2 tablespoons lemon juice
Hot cooked rice

1. In 10-inch skillet over medium heat, in hot oil, cook chops about 10 minutes or until browned on both sides. Remove chops; set aside and keep warm. Reserve drippings in skillet.

2. Add onion, basil and pepper to skillet. Cook 2 minutes, stirring often. Stir in soup and water until smooth. Heat to boiling. Add chops and sliced orange. Reduce heat to low. Cover; simmer 5 minutes.

3. Add green pepper. Cover; simmer 5 minutes more or until chops are tender and green pepper is tender-crisp. Stir in lemon juice. Serve chops and sauce over rice. Makes 6 servings.

Spiced Pork Loin with
Sweet Potatoes

Mushroom-Stuffed Ham

6 tablespoons butter or
   margarine
4 packages (8 ounces *each*)
   Campbell's Fresh mushrooms,
   finely chopped (about
   10 cups)
½ cup finely chopped onion
2 cups soft bread crumbs
2 tablespoons chopped fresh
   parsley

1 teaspoon grated orange peel
¼ teaspoon ground nutmeg
   Dash pepper
7- to 8-pound fully cooked
   smoked shank half ham
½ cup orange marmalade
1 tablespoon frozen orange juice
   concentrate

1. To make stuffing: In 10-inch skillet over medium heat, in hot butter, cook mushrooms and onion until tender and liquid is evaporated, stirring occasionally. Add crumbs, parsley, orange peel, nutmeg and pepper.

2. Remove rind from ham; trim excess fat. Slice ham to bone at 1-inch intervals. Spoon stuffing between each slice. Place ham on rack in roasting pan; cover with foil. Bake at 325°F. about 2 hours or until thoroughly heated.

3. Meanwhile, in small saucepan, heat marmalade and orange juice concentrate until melted. During last 30 minutes of baking, brush ham often with marmalade mixture. Makes 12 servings.

Pineapple-Glazed Ham and Sweet Potatoes

1 can (8 ounces) pineapple slices
   in juice, undrained
1 package (12 ounces) Mrs. Paul's
   frozen candied sweet
   potatoes

1 tablespoon Dijon-style mustard
3 slices fully cooked ham, each
   cut about ⅜ inch thick
   (¾ pound)

1. Drain pineapple, reserving *⅓ cup* of the juice. In 10-inch skillet, stir together reserved juice, candied sauce mix, sweet potatoes and mustard. Over medium heat, heat to boiling. Reduce heat to low. Cover; simmer 20 minutes, stirring often.

2. Add ham slices and pineapple. Cover and cook 5 minutes more or until potatoes are tender. Makes 3 servings.

TO MICROWAVE: Drain pineapple, reserving *2 tablespoons* of the juice. To make sauce: In small bowl, stir together reserved juice, candied sauce mix and mustard. Arrange ham slices in center of 10-inch microwave-safe pie plate. Cut pineapple slices in half; arrange pineapple and sweet potatoes around edge of dish. Spoon sauce over. Cover with vented plastic wrap; microwave on HIGH 10 minutes or until potatoes are tender, rotating dish twice during cooking. Spoon sauce over ham and potatoes to serve.

Spicy Chicken and Vegetables

4 whole chicken leg quarters
½ teaspoon salt
½ teaspoon pepper
2 tablespoons vegetable oil
8 ounces smoked sausage,
    diagonally cut into
    1-inch pieces
2 medium onions, coarsely
    chopped
2 cloves garlic, minced

1 can (8 ounces) tomato sauce
¼ cup water
1 tablespoon peanut butter
⅛ teaspoon ground red pepper
1 package (20 ounces) Mrs. Paul's
    frozen candied sweet
    potatoes
1 pound (½ of medium head)
    cabbage, cut into 8 wedges
Hot cooked rice

1. Cut each chicken leg to separate thigh and drumstick. Sprinkle chicken with salt and pepper. In 6-quart Dutch oven over medium heat, in hot oil, cook chicken pieces, *half* at a time, until browned, removing chicken pieces as they brown. Spoon off fat.

2. Add sausage, onions and garlic; cook 3 minutes, stirring often. Stir in tomato sauce, water, peanut butter and red pepper; heat to boiling. Return chicken to Dutch oven. Reduce heat to low. Cover; simmer 20 minutes, stirring occasionally. Push chicken to one side of Dutch oven.

3. Add sweet potatoes and candied sauce mix; rearrange chicken. Cover; simmer 10 minutes more.

4. Add cabbage, pushing into liquid; cover and simmer 20 minutes more or until chicken is tender and juices run clear and potatoes are tender. Remove chicken, sausage, potatoes and cabbage to serving platter. Spoon some sauce over all; serve remaining sauce with rice. Makes 8 servings.

Chicken Broccoli Pasta Parmesan

2 tablespoons vegetable oil
1 pound boneless, skinless
    chicken breasts, cut
    into cubes
¼ cup chopped onion
1 can (10¾ ounces) Campbell's
    condensed cream of broccoli
    soup

2 tablespoons milk
1 tablespoon dry sherry
1 cup sliced Campbell's Fresh
    mushrooms
1 cup cooked broccoli flowerets
½ cup grated Parmesan cheese
Hot cooked spaghetti

1. In 10-inch skillet over medium heat, in hot oil, cook chicken and onion until chicken is browned and onion is tender, stirring often.

2. Stir in soup, milk and sherry until smooth. Add mushrooms, broccoli and Parmesan. Reduce heat to low. Cover; simmer 10 minutes, stirring occasionally. Serve over spaghetti. Top with additional Parmesan, if desired. Makes 4 cups or 4 servings.

Herb-Stuffed Turkey

Let your imagination go when it comes to garnishing the holiday turkey. Pictured opposite and on back cover.

1 can (14½ ounces) Swanson clear ready to serve chicken broth
2 cups chopped onions
1 cup sliced celery
½ cup diced carrots
2 tablespoons butter or margarine
2 tablespoons chopped fresh parsley
½ teaspoon dried thyme leaves, crushed
⅛ teaspoon pepper

2 eggs
3 cups herb seasoned stuffing mix
2 cups coarsely crushed cracked-wheat crackers (about 20 crackers)
14- to 16-pound fresh or frozen turkey, thawed
2 cans (10½ ounces *each*) Franco-American turkey gravy
Seckel pears, cranberries, kale, lemon leaves and fresh herbs for garnish

1. In 2-quart saucepan over medium heat, heat broth, onions, celery and carrots to boiling. Reduce heat to low. Cover; simmer 10 minutes. Drain, reserving *1¼ cups* of the cooking liquid.

2. Meanwhile, in same saucepan over medium heat, heat butter, parsley, thyme and pepper until butter is melted.

3. In large bowl, beat eggs. Add stuffing mix, crushed crackers and drained vegetables. Add the reserved liquid and melted butter mixture; toss gently to mix.

4. Remove neck and giblets from inside turkey. Remove excess fat. Cut off and discard neck skin. Rinse turkey with cold running water; drain well. Spoon stuffing loosely into body and neck cavities. Fold skin over stuffing; skewer closed. Tie legs with kitchen string. Place turkey, breast side up, on rack in roasting pan. Lift wings toward neck, then fold tips under back of turkey to balance. Insert meat thermometer into thickest part of meat between breast and thigh, without touching fat or bone.

5. Roast at 325°F. for 4½ to 5½ hours or until internal temperature reaches 180°F. and drumstick moves easily when twisted and juices run clear. Baste every 30 minutes with pan drippings. When turkey skin turns golden, cover loosely with tent of foil. Begin checking for doneness after 3 hours.

6. Transfer turkey to cutting board, reserving pan drippings. Let turkey stand, covered, 20 minutes for easier carving. Skim fat from drippings. Stir *1½ cups* of the drippings and the gravy into roasting pan. Over medium heat, heat to boiling, stirring to loosen browned bits; serve gravy with turkey and stuffing. Garnish with seckel pears, cranberries, kale, lemon leaves and fresh herbs, if desired. Makes 14 to 16 servings.

Herb-Stuffed Turkey

Artichoke-Stuffed Chicken Breasts

Serve baby carrots with these company-special chicken rolls. Pictured opposite.

2 cups shredded Jarlsberg cheese (8 ounces)
1 teaspoon paprika
½ teaspoon dry mustard
¼ teaspoon dried thyme leaves, crushed
4 whole chicken breasts, split, skinned and boned (about 2 pounds boneless)
1 can (about 14 ounces) artichoke hearts, rinsed, drained and quartered

¼ cup Chablis or other dry white wine
1 tablespoon butter or margarine
1 cup sliced Campbell's Fresh mushrooms
⅛ teaspoon dried thyme leaves, crushed
1 can (10½ ounces) Franco-American chicken gravy
1 tablespoon chopped fresh parsley

1. In bowl, combine cheese, paprika, mustard and the ¼ teaspoon thyme.

2. Place each chicken breast between sheets of plastic wrap. With meat mallet or rolling pin, pound each chicken breast half to ¼-inch thickness. Divide artichoke quarters among chicken breasts; place *1 tablespoon* of the cheese mixture in center of *each* chicken breast half. Roll up chicken from short end, jelly-roll fashion. Secure with short skewers, if necessary.

3. Place chicken rolls, seam side down, in 12- by 8-inch baking dish. Press remaining cheese mixture on top of each chicken roll. Pour wine into dish. Bake at 350°F. for 35 minutes or until chicken is tender and juices run clear. Transfer chicken to platter; keep warm. Reserve ¼ *cup* of the drippings.

4. Meanwhile, in 2-quart saucepan over medium heat, in hot butter, cook mushrooms and the ⅛ teaspoon thyme until mushrooms are tender, stirring often. Add gravy, parsley and reserved drippings; heat through. Serve over chicken rolls. Makes 8 servings.

TO MICROWAVE: Prepare chicken rolls as directed in steps 1 and 2. Place chicken rolls, seam side down, in 12- by 8-inch microwave-safe baking dish. Pour wine into dish. Cover with waxed paper. Microwave on HIGH 12 minutes or until chicken is tender and juices run clear, rotating dish twice during cooking. Remove waxed paper. Press remaining cheese mixture on top of each chicken roll. Let stand, uncovered, 5 minutes. Transfer chicken to platter; keep warm. Reserve ¼ *cup* of the drippings; set aside.

In 1-quart microwave-safe casserole, combine butter, mushrooms and thyme. Cover with lid; microwave on HIGH 3 minutes or until mushrooms are tender, stirring once during cooking. Stir in gravy, parsley and reserved drippings. Cover; microwave on HIGH 2 minutes or until sauce is hot, stirring once during cooking. Makes 8 servings.

Artichoke-Stuffed
Chicken Breasts

Lemon Garlic Shrimp

A colorful and surprisingly easy main dish that will impress dinner guests. Pictured opposite.

1 can (14½ ounces) Swanson clear ready to serve chicken broth
2 tablespoons cornstarch
2 tablespoons olive oil
4 cloves garlic, minced
¼ teaspoon grated lemon peel
⅛ teaspoon ground red pepper

1½ pounds medium shrimp, shelled and deveined (about 54)
¼ cup chopped fresh parsley
2 tablespoons lemon juice
6 cups hot cooked spaghetti (12 ounces uncooked)
Freshly ground black pepper

1. In bowl, stir broth into cornstarch; set aside.

2. In 10-inch skillet over medium heat, in hot oil, cook garlic, lemon peel and red pepper 1 minute, stirring constantly. Add shrimp, parsley and lemon juice. Cook until shrimp are pink, stirring often. Gradually stir in broth mixture. Over medium heat, cook until mixture boils and thickens, stirring constantly. Toss with spaghetti. Serve with freshly ground black pepper. Makes 8 cups or 6 servings.

TO MICROWAVE: Reduce garlic to 3 cloves. In 2-cup glass measure, stir broth into cornstarch. Microwave, uncovered, on HIGH 4 minutes or until mixture boils and thickens, stirring after each minute. Cover; set aside.

In 2-quart microwave-safe casserole, combine oil, 3 cloves garlic, lemon peel and red pepper. Cover with lid; microwave on HIGH 1 minute. Stir in shrimp, parsley and lemon juice. Cover; microwave on HIGH 3 minutes or until most shrimp are pink, stirring once during cooking. Stir in broth mixture. Cover; microwave on HIGH 2 minutes more or until mixture boils and thickens, stirring after each minute. Toss with spaghetti. Serve with freshly ground black pepper.

Fish with Tangy Mustard Sauce

The creamy mustard sauce makes a zesty topper for fish fillets.

1 package (9 ounces) Mrs. Paul's frozen prepared light fillets (haddock or cod)
½ cup sour cream

1 tablespoon spicy brown mustard
6 drops hot pepper sauce

1. Remove create-a-sauce seasoning packet from fish; set aside. Bake fish according to package directions.

2. Meanwhile, in bowl, stir together sour cream, mustard, pepper sauce and contents of create-a-sauce packet. Serve with fish. Makes 2 servings.

Lemon Garlic Shrimp

Fish with Caper Salsa

This tangy salsa gives simple fish fillets a contemporary twist.

1 medium Campbell's Fresh tomato, chopped	1 tablespoon olive oil
2 tablespoons sliced green onion	1 package (9 ounces) Mrs. Paul's frozen prepared light fillets
1 tablespoon Vlasic capers	(haddock, cod or flounder)
1 tablespoon vinegar	

1. To make salsa: In small bowl, combine tomato, onion, capers, vinegar and oil. Toss to mix well. Cover; refrigerate at least 4 hours to blend flavors.

2. Bake fish according to package directions, reserving create-a-sauce seasoning packet for another use. Serve salsa with fish. Makes 2 servings.

Turkey Gravy Dijon

Add cubed cooked turkey or chicken to this piquant sauce to make a shortcut version of creamed turkey to spoon over toast triangles, hot cooked pasta or rice.

1 can (10½ ounces) Franco-American turkey gravy	2 teaspoons Dijon-style mustard
2 tablespoons milk	¼ cup shredded Swiss cheese (1 ounce)

In 1½-quart saucepan, stir together gravy, milk and mustard. Over medium heat, heat until warm, stirring often. Add cheese; cook until cheese melts, stirring constantly. *Do not boil.* Serve with turkey or rice. Makes about 1 cup.

TO MICROWAVE: In 4-cup glass measure or 1-quart microwave-safe casserole, stir together gravy, milk and mustard. Microwave, uncovered, on HIGH 4 minutes or until heated through, stirring once during cooking. Stir in cheese. Microwave on MEDIUM (50% power) 2 to 3 minutes or until cheese melts, stirring twice during cooking. *Do not boil.* Serve as directed above.

Buttermilk Chicken Gravy

Buttermilk adds a tangy richness to ready-to-heat chicken gravy. Serve Buttermilk Chicken Gravy with fried chicken and biscuits for a tasty Southern-style meal.

1 can (10½ ounces) Franco-American chicken gravy	¼ cup buttermilk or plain yogurt
⅛ teaspoon dried rosemary leaves, crushed	1 tablespoon finely chopped fresh parsley

In 1½-quart saucepan over medium heat, heat gravy and rosemary until warm. Stir in buttermilk and parsley. Heat through, stirring occasionally. *Do not boil.* Serve immediately with chicken. Makes about 1¼ cups.

Garden Vegetable Gravy

This chunky vegetable-studded gravy enhances most beef cuts. When you have leftovers, spoon it over hot roast beef sandwiches or use as the base for a homestyle beef pot pie.

1 tablespoon butter or margarine	1 can (about 8 ounces) tomatoes, undrained, cut up
½ cup finely chopped onion	1 can (10¼ ounces) Franco-American beef gravy
¼ cup finely chopped celery	
¼ teaspoon dried thyme leaves, crushed	

1. In 2-quart saucepan over medium heat, in hot butter, cook onion, celery and thyme about 5 minutes or until onion is tender, stirring occasionally. Stir in tomatoes with their liquid. Cover; simmer 15 minutes or until celery is tender.

2. Stir in gravy. Heat through, stirring occasionally. Serve with beef. Makes about 2 cups.

TO MICROWAVE: In 1½-quart microwave-safe casserole, combine butter, onion, celery and thyme. Cover with lid; microwave on HIGH 5 minutes or until onion is tender, stirring once during cooking. Stir in tomatoes with their liquid. Cover; microwave on HIGH 7 to 9 minutes or until celery is tender, stirring twice during cooking. Stir in gravy. Cover; microwave on HIGH 2 to 3 minutes more or until hot, stirring once during cooking.

Shiitake Wine Sauce

The enticing flavors of shiitake mushrooms and tarragon make a delicious flavor combination. Serve with beef or pork.

1 package (3½ ounces) Campbell's Fresh shiitake mushrooms	¼ cup Chablis or other dry white wine
3 tablespoons butter or margarine	1 can (10¼ ounces) Franco-American beef gravy
3 tablespoons chopped shallots	½ cup tomato sauce
¼ teaspoon dried tarragon leaves, crushed	2 tablespoons chopped fresh parsley

1. Trim woody portions of mushroom stems and discard. Chop mushrooms.

2. In 10-inch skillet over medium heat, in hot butter, cook mushrooms, shallots and tarragon until mushrooms are tender, stirring occasionally.

3. Add wine; cook until most of liquid is evaporated. Add gravy and tomato sauce. Heat through, stirring occasionally.

4. Stir in parsley just before serving. Makes about 1¾ cups sauce.

Holiday Planned-Overs

Turn your leftover turkey or ham into special main dishes that taste just as good the second time around. Look for saucy Tortellini with Mushrooms and Ham or spectacular Beef Paprikash with Noodles. Serve hearty Sweet Potato Shepherd's Pie or Turkey-and-Stuffing au Gratin for a delicious family meal. These meal-time creations are enhanced with fresh seasonings and use subtle ethnic touches that turn everyday leftovers into delicious entrées bound to become new family favorites.

Beef Paprikash with Noodles

Beef Paprikash
with Noodles

Well seasoned with paprika, Worcestershire sauce and onion, this hearty meal goes together fast because you start with leftover cooked roast beef. Pictured opposite.

　2 **tablespoons butter or margarine**
　1 **package (8 ounces) Campbell's Fresh mushrooms, sliced**
　1 **medium onion, chopped**
　1 **clove garlic, minced**
　1 **tablespoon paprika**
　2 **cans (14½ ounces *each*) Swanson clear ready to serve beef broth**
　1 **can (6 ounces) tomato paste**
　1 **tablespoon Worcestershire sauce**
½ **teaspoon sugar**
⅛ **teaspoon pepper**
　2 **cups cubed cooked beef Hot cooked wide noodles**

1. In 10-inch skillet over medium heat, in hot butter, cook mushrooms, onion, garlic and paprika until onion is tender, stirring often.

2. Stir in broth, tomato paste, Worcestershire, sugar and pepper. Simmer over medium heat 25 minutes or until sauce thickens, stirring occasionally.

3. Stir in beef; heat through. Serve over noodles. Makes 4½ cups or 4 servings.

Nacho Turkey Puff

This colorful, Southwestern-style casserole is a tasty choice to serve at a holiday brunch, luncheon or dinner.

2 tablespoons vegetable oil
1 cup chopped onions
1 cup chopped green pepper
2 cloves garlic, minced
1 teaspoon ground cumin
1 can (11 ounces) Campbell's condensed nacho cheese soup/dip, divided

3 cups shredded cooked turkey or chicken
¼ cup water
3 eggs, separated
1 can (17 ounces) whole kernel golden corn, drained
Sour cream (optional)

1. Preheat oven to 350°F. Grease 12- by 8-inch baking dish. In 10-inch skillet over medium heat, in hot oil, cook onions, green pepper, garlic and cumin until vegetables are tender, stirring often.

2. Stir in *½ cup* of the soup, the turkey and water. Cook until heated through, stirring often. Spoon into prepared baking dish.

3. In medium bowl with mixer at medium speed, beat egg whites until stiff peaks form. In small bowl, stir remaining soup and the corn into egg yolks. Fold egg yolk mixture into whites. Spoon over chicken mixture. Bake 30 minutes or until topping is puffy and browned. Serve with sour cream, if desired. Makes 6 to 8 servings.

Turkey-and-Stuffing au Gratin

2 cups cubed cooked turkey or chicken
2 cups seasoned cubed stuffing mix
1 can (10½ ounces) Franco-American turkey gravy

1 cup thinly sliced celery
1 cup shredded Cheddar cheese (4 ounces), divided
¼ cup chopped onion
Generous dash pepper

1. In large bowl, combine turkey, stuffing mix, gravy, celery, ½ cup of the cheese, the onion and pepper. Spoon into 10- by 6-inch baking dish.

2. Bake at 350°F. for 35 minutes or until heated through. Sprinkle with remaining cheese. Bake 10 minutes more or until cheese is melted. Makes 5 cups or 5 servings.

TO MICROWAVE: In 10- by 6-inch microwave-safe baking dish, combine *¼ cup* of the gravy, celery and onion. Cover with vented plastic wrap; microwave on HIGH 5 minutes or until celery and onion are tender, stirring once during cooking. Stir in turkey, stuffing, mix remaining gravy and *½ cup* of the cheese and the pepper. Cover; microwave on HIGH 5 to 8 minutes or until heated through, stirring twice during cooking. Top with remaining cheese. Let stand, covered, 5 minutes before serving.

Sweet Potato Shepherd's Pie

Choose your family's favorite vegetable when you make this easy-on-the-cook casserole.

1 package (20 ounces) Mrs. Paul's
    frozen candied sweet
    potatoes
2 tablespoons lemon juice
½ teaspoon rubbed sage, divided
1 can (10½ ounces) Franco-
    American turkey gravy

3 cups diced, cooked turkey or
    chicken
3 cups cooked, drained,
    vegetables (such as chopped
    broccoli, Italian-style green
    beans, corn or sliced carrots)

1. Prepare sweet potatoes according to package directions. With potato masher, mash until smooth. Stir in lemon juice and *¼ teaspoon* of the sage; set aside.

2. Preheat oven to 400°F. In 2-quart casserole, stir together gravy, turkey, vegetables and remaining sage.

3. Spoon potato mixture on top; spread to edges. Bake 25 minutes or until hot and bubbling. Makes 6 servings.

Turkey-Broccoli Divan

1 package (10 ounces) frozen
    broccoli spears, cooked and
    drained
1½ cups cubed cooked turkey or
    chicken
1 can (10¾ ounces) Campbell's
    condensed cream of
    broccoli soup

⅓ cup milk
½ cup shredded Cheddar cheese
    (2 ounces)
2 tablespoons dry bread crumbs
1 tablespoon butter or margarine,
    melted

1. Preheat oven to 450°F. In 10- by 6-inch baking dish, arrange broccoli; top with turkey. In medium bowl, stir together soup and milk until smooth; pour over turkey. Sprinkle with cheese.

2. In cup, combine bread crumbs and butter; sprinkle over cheese. Bake 15 minutes or until hot. Makes 4 servings.

TO MICROWAVE: In 10- by 6-inch microwave-safe baking dish, arrange broccoli. Top with turkey. In medium bowl, stir together soup and milk until smooth; pour over turkey. Sprinkle with cheese. Cover with waxed paper; microwave on HIGH 6 minutes or until heated through, rotating dish halfway through cooking. In cup, combine bread crumbs and butter; sprinkle over cheese. Microwave, uncovered, on HIGH 1 minute. Let stand 5 minutes before serving.

Mediterranean-Style Fettuccine

For variety, try one of the many kinds of fettuccine available today. Tomato-flavored pasta was used in this photo. Pictured opposite.

2 tablespoons olive oil
¼ cup sliced green onions
1 clove garlic, minced
½ teaspoon dried oregano
   leaves, crushed
1 medium zucchini, halved
   lengthwise and sliced
2 Campbell's Fresh tomatoes,
   chopped
3 cups cubed cooked turkey or
   chicken

1 can (10½ ounces) Franco-
   American chicken gravy
½ cup Swanson clear ready to
   serve chicken broth
4 cups hot cooked fettuccine
   (8 ounces uncooked)
Sliced Vlasic ripe olives and
   crumbled feta cheese for
   garnish

1. In 2-quart saucepan over medium heat, in hot oil, cook onions, garlic and oregano about 3 minutes or until onions are tender, stirring occasionally. Add zucchini; cook 2 minutes. Stir in tomatoes, turkey, gravy and broth. Heat through, stirring occasionally.

2. In large bowl, pour turkey mixture over fettuccine; toss lightly to coat. Garnish with olives and feta cheese, if desired. Makes 8 cups or 6 servings.

Caraway Turkey-Noodle Bake

6 cups wide egg noodles,
   uncooked (8 ounces)
2 cups coarsely chopped cabbage
½ cup diced carrots
3 cups diced cooked turkey or
   chicken
1 can (10½ ounces) Franco-
   American chicken gravy

½ cup sour cream
3 slices bacon, cooked and
   crumbled
4 teaspoons spicy brown
   mustard
½ teaspoon caraway seed
½ cup shredded Swiss cheese
   (2 ounces)

1. Preheat oven to 400°F. Cook noodles with cabbage and carrots according to noodle package directions; drain.

2. Meanwhile, in bowl, combine turkey, gravy, sour cream, bacon, mustard and caraway. Add noodle mixture; toss. Spoon into 2-quart casserole. Bake 20 minutes or until heated through. Top with cheese. Bake 5 minutes more or until cheese is melted. Makes 8 cups or 8 servings.

TO MICROWAVE: Prepare noodles, cabbage and carrots as directed in step 1. In 3-quart microwave-safe casserole, combine turkey, gravy, sour cream, bacon, mustard and caraway. Cover with lid; microwave on HIGH 2 minutes. Stir in noodle mixture. Cover; microwave on HIGH 7 minutes or until heated through, stirring once during cooking. Top with cheese. Microwave, uncovered, on HIGH 2 minutes or until cheese is melted.

Mediterranean-Style Fettuccine

Turkey and Dumplings

Fluffy sour cream dumplings cook on top a savory turkey stew for a hearty one-dish meal.

2 tablespoons butter or margarine
½ cup chopped carrot
½ cup chopped onion
½ teaspoon dried basil leaves, crushed
⅛ teaspoon pepper
2 cups cubed cooked turkey or chicken
1 can (10¾ ounces) Campbell's condensed cream of mushroom, creamy chicken mushroom or cream of chicken soup

1 soup can milk
1 cup packaged biscuit mix
½ cup sour cream
2 tablespoons chopped fresh parsley

1. In 10-inch skillet over medium heat, in hot butter, cook carrot, onion, basil and pepper until vegetables are tender, stirring occasionally.

2. Stir in turkey, soup and milk. Heat to boiling. Reduce heat to low. Cover; simmer 5 minutes, stirring occasionally.

3. Meanwhile, in small bowl, stir together biscuit mix, sour cream and parsley until just blended. Drop by spoonfuls onto hot turkey mixture, making 8 dumplings. Simmer, uncovered, 10 minutes. Cover; simmer 10 minutes more or until wooden toothpick inserted in center of dumpling comes out clean. Makes 4 servings.

Ginger-Turkey Spaghetti

2 cans (14½ ounces *each*) Swanson clear ready to serve chicken broth
2 cups shredded cooked turkey or chicken
¼ cup orange juice
2 tablespoons soy sauce
½ teaspoon ground ginger

¼ teaspoon garlic powder
8 ounces thin spaghetti, uncooked and broken up
1 package (16 ounces) frozen mixed Oriental vegetables
4 teaspoons water
4 teaspoons cornstarch

1. In 4-quart saucepan over medium heat, heat broth, turkey, orange juice, soy sauce, ginger and garlic powder to boiling. Add spaghetti and vegetables. Cook 7 minutes or until spaghetti is done, stirring occasionally.

2. In cup, stir water into cornstarch. Stir into saucepan. Cook 2 minutes or until mixture boils and thickens, stirring constantly. Makes 6 cups or 4 servings.

Caper Turkey Salad Sandwiches

Serve the turkey filling on lettuce leaves or tomato slices for salads instead of sandwiches.

**2 cups chopped cooked turkey
    or chicken**
I cup thinly sliced celery
⅓ cup mayonnaise
**2 tablespoons finely chopped
    onion**
**I tablespoon Vlasic capers,
    chopped**

⅛ teaspoon pepper
8 slices bread
   **Campbell's Fresh butterhead
    lettuce leaves**
**2 Campbell's Fresh tomatoes,
    sliced**

1. In medium bowl, combine turkey, celery, mayonnaise, onion, capers and pepper; toss to mix well.

2. On each of 4 bread slices, layer lettuce, then ¼ of the turkey mixture and ¼ of the tomato slices. Top with remaining bread. Press lightly; cut in half. Makes 4 sandwiches or 2½ cups mixture.

Red Beans and Rice

A little holiday ham goes a long way when you combine it with beans and rice and spicy Cajun-style seasonings.

2 tablespoons vegetable oil
I cup chopped onions
**I cup coarsely chopped green
    pepper**
I clove garlic, minced
**½ teaspoon dried thyme leaves,
    crushed**
**I can (14½ ounces) Swanson
    clear ready to serve
    beef broth**

I bay leaf
**¾ cup regular long-grain rice,
    uncooked**
I cup diced cooked ham
**I can (16 ounces) red kidney or
    pinto beans, drained**
¼ teaspoon hot pepper sauce

1. In 3-quart saucepan over medium heat, in hot oil, cook onions, pepper, garlic and thyme 3 minutes, stirring occasionally.

2. Stir in broth and bay leaf; heat to boiling. Stir in rice. Reduce heat to low. Cover; simmer 10 minutes.

3. Stir in ham, beans and hot pepper sauce. Cover; simmer 10 minutes more or until liquid is almost absorbed. Remove from heat. Let stand, covered, 5 minutes.

4. Remove bay leaf; discard. Serve with additional hot pepper sauce, if desired. Makes 5 cups or 5 servings.

Tortellini with Mushrooms and Ham

Adding a simple but colorful garnish can make an everyday entrée look special. Pictured opposite.

1 tablespoon olive oil
½ cup cooked ham, cut into strips
¼ cup chopped onion
1 clove garlic, minced
½ teaspoon dried basil leaves, crushed
1 can (10¾ ounces) Campbell's condensed cream of mushroom soup
1 cup frozen peas

1 soup can milk
2 tablespoons chopped fresh parsley
⅛ teaspoon pepper
3 cups hot cooked cheese tortellini (2½ cups uncooked)
Grated Parmesan cheese
Cherry tomatoes, curly endive, sweet red pepper rings and Italian parsley for garnish

1. In 2-quart saucepan over medium heat, in hot oil, cook ham, onion, garlic and basil 2 minutes, stirring often.

2. Stir in soup and peas; heat to boiling. Reduce heat to low. Cover; simmer 5 minutes or until peas are tender.

3. Stir in milk, parsley and pepper; heat through. In large bowl, pour soup mixture over tortellini; toss lightly to coat. Serve with Parmesan. Garnish with cherry tomatoes, endive, red pepper and parsley, if desired. Makes 4 cups or 4 servings.

Ham with Cornmeal Biscuits

This homestyle casserole will chase the chill away on a cold winter's evening.

1 package (10 ounces) frozen succotash
1 medium onion, chopped
2 cans (10½ ounces *each*) Franco-American golden pork gravy
1½ cups cooked ham cut into 2- by ½-inch strips

1 tablespoon spicy brown mustard
1 cup packaged biscuit mix
½ cup cornmeal
⅔ cup milk

1. Cook succotash and onion according to succotash package directions; drain. Preheat oven to 425°F.

2. In 2-quart casserole, stir together gravy, ham, mustard and succotash mixture.

3. In medium bowl, stir together biscuit mix and cornmeal. Stir in milk until just blended. Drop by spoonfuls onto ham mixture, making 8 biscuits.

4. Bake 25 minutes or until biscuits are golden brown and ham mixture is hot and bubbling. Makes 4 servings.

Tortellini with Mushrooms and Ham

Holiday Breakfasts and Brunches

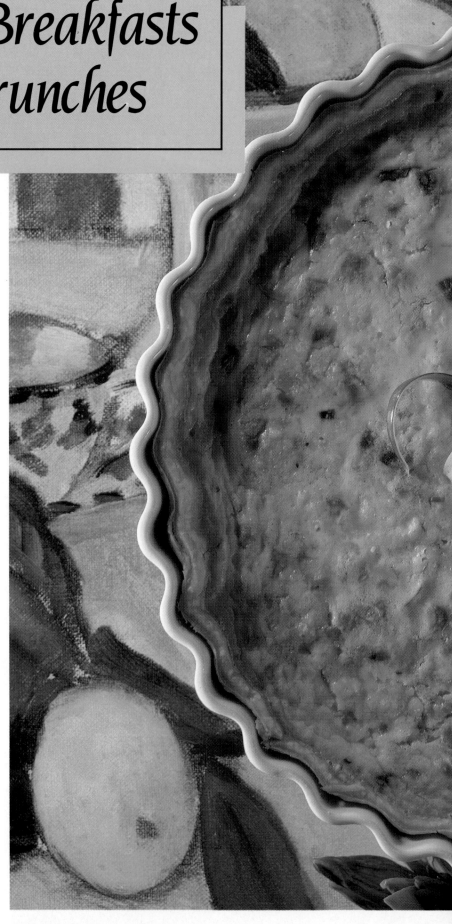

Brunch is a smart, and easy, way to entertain guests during the holidays. Welcome guests with a pitcher of chilled V8 vegetable juice or a colorful fruit compote plus one of these scrumptious entrées for a welcome change of pace. You'll find lots of ways to prepare eggs and cheese in fluffy omelets, light soufflés, easy-to-make casseroles and even a delicate mushroom quiche. Round out the morning feast with traditional cheese grits, spicy sweet potato muffins or a cheesy spoon bread for a memorable and easy meal.

Mushroom Quiche

Mushroom Quiche

You can purchase edible flowers in gourmet food shops or florists or grow them yourself. Be sure they're pesticide-free. Pictured opposite.

    9-inch unbaked piecrust
2 tablespoons butter or margarine
**1 package (12 ounces) Campbell's
    Fresh mushrooms, chopped
    (about 4 cups)**
¼ cup chopped green onions
⅛ teaspoon ground nutmeg
4 eggs
¾ cup milk
¾ cup light cream
**1 cup shredded Swiss cheese
    (4 ounces)**
1 tablespoon all-purpose flour
1 teaspoon lemon juice
⅛ teaspoon pepper
**Green onion strips and fresh
    edible flowers for garnish**

1. Preheat oven to 450°F. Line inside of piecrust with foil; fill with uncooked rice or dried beans. Bake 10 minutes. Remove foil and rice; cool slightly. Reduce oven temperature to 375°F.

2. Meanwhile, in 10-inch skillet over medium-high heat, in hot butter, cook mushrooms, onions and nutmeg until mushrooms are tender and liquid is evaporated, stirring occasionally.

3. In large bowl, beat eggs. Stir in milk, cream, cheese, flour, lemon juice and pepper. Stir in mushroom mixture. Pour into piecrust.

4. Bake 35 minutes or until knife inserted in center comes out clean. Let stand on wire rack 5 minutes before serving. Garnish with green onion strips and edible flowers, if desired. Makes 6 servings.

Potato-Egg Pie

4 eggs
1 can (10¾ ounces) Campbell's
  condensed cream of celery
  soup
¼ cup milk
1 cup shredded Cheddar cheese
  (4 ounces)

1 medium potato, peeled and
  shredded (about ¾ cup)
2 slices bacon, cooked and
  crumbled
¼ cup sliced green onions

1. Grease 9-inch pie plate. In large bowl with mixer at medium speed, beat eggs until foamy. Gradually stir in soup and milk. Stir in cheese, potato, bacon and onions.

2. Pour into prepared pie plate. Bake at 350°F. for 40 minutes or until knife inserted in center comes out clean. Let stand on wire rack 10 minutes before serving. Makes 6 servings.

Tortilla Egg Bake

Give your brunch a Mexican theme. Serve this zesty egg casserole with a colorful fruit salad of oranges, pineapple and grapes sprinkled with pomegranate seeds.

Vegetable oil
6 (6-inch) flour tortillas
1 can (11 ounces) Campbell's
  condensed zesty tomato
  soup
10 eggs
1 cup shredded Monterey Jack
  cheese with jalapeno
  peppers (4 ounces), divided

½ pound bulk pork sausage,
  cooked, drained and
  crumbled
1 can (4 ounces) chopped green
  chilies, drained
¼ cup finely chopped onion
½ teaspoon chili powder
1 avocado, sliced

1. Grease 12- by 8-inch baking dish. In 10-inch skillet over medium heat, in ½-inch hot oil, fry tortillas, one at a time, 2 to 3 seconds on each side to soften. Drain on paper towels.

2. Arrange tortillas over bottom and halfway up sides of prepared baking dish.

3. In medium bowl, stir soup until smooth; beat in eggs. Stir in *½ cup* of the cheese, the sausage, green chilies, onion and chili powder. Pour *immediately* over tortillas.

4. Bake at 350°F. for 35 minutes or until knife inserted in center comes out clean. Top with remaining cheese and the avocado slices. Makes 8 servings.

Nacho Broccoli Strata

This is sure to be a hit with the children at your breakfast table — even those who don't like vegetables.

6 cups stale white bread cut into 1-inch cubes
2 cups cooked broccoli flowerets or 1 package (10 ounces) frozen broccoli spears, thawed, drained and cut up

1 can (11 ounces) Campbell's condensed nacho cheese soup/dip
2 cups milk
2 cups shredded Monterey Jack cheese (8 ounces)
5 eggs, beaten

1. Grease 12- by 8-inch baking dish. Arrange bread cubes and broccoli evenly in prepared dish.

2. In large bowl, stir together soup, milk, cheese and eggs; mix well. Pour over bread and broccoli. Cover; refrigerate 2 hours or overnight.

3. Uncover. Bake at 350°F. for 40 minutes or until knife inserted in center comes out clean. Let stand on wire rack 10 minutes before serving. Makes 6 servings.

Two-Cheese Soufflé

Using canned soup as a base makes this cheese soufflé deceptively simple.

1 can (11 ounces) Campbell's condensed Cheddar cheese soup/sauce
½ cup shredded Swiss cheese (2 ounces)

1 tablespoon chopped fresh dill or ½ teaspoon dried dill weed, crushed
6 eggs, separated

1. In 2-quart saucepan, combine soup, cheese and dill. Cook over medium-low heat until cheese melts, stirring often; set aside.

2. In large bowl with mixer at high speed, beat egg whites until stiff peaks form.

3. Blend egg yolks into soup mixture. Gently fold soup mixture into beaten whites.

4. Pour into *ungreased* 2-quart casserole or soufflé dish. Bake at 350°F. for 35 to 45 minutes or until lightly browned. Serve immediately. Makes 6 servings.

Omelet Primavera

Serve with Spiced Sweet Potato Muffins (see page 58). Pictured opposite.

1 can (10½ ounces) Franco-
   American chicken gravy,
   divided
5 tablespoons butter or
   margarine, divided
1 small onion, sliced and
   separated into rings

1 medium green pepper, cut into
   2-inch-long strips
1 can (about 16 ounces) tomatoes,
   drained, cut up
¼ teaspoon pepper, divided
6 eggs
⅓ cup shredded Cheddar cheese

1. Reserve ⅓ *cup* of the gravy; set aside. To make vegetable sauce: In 2-quart saucepan over medium heat, in *2 tablespoons* hot butter, cook onion and green pepper until tender-crisp, stirring often. Stir in remaining gravy, tomatoes and ⅛ *teaspoon* of the pepper; heat through, stirring occasionally. Keep warm.

2. To make omelet: In medium bowl, beat eggs. Stir in reserved ⅓ *cup* gravy and remaining pepper. In 10-inch nonstick omelet pan or skillet over medium-high heat, melt *1 tablespoon* of the remaining butter. Pour ⅓ of the egg mixture into pan. Lift edges as eggs set, tilting skillet to allow uncooked egg mixture to flow underneath.

3. When omelet is set but still moist, spoon ⅓ *cup* of the vegetable sauce over *half* of omelet. Top with ⅓ of the cheese. Fold omelet over filling; slide onto warm plate. Repeat steps 2 and 3 to make 2 more omelets. Serve omelets with remaining vegetable sauce. Makes 3 servings.

Campbelled Eggs

This soup-and-egg classic can also be made with cream of celery, cream of mushroom, cream of potato, Cheddar cheese or nacho cheese soup.

1 can (10¾ ounces) Campbell's
   condensed cream of chicken
   soup
8 eggs
   Dash pepper

2 tablespoons butter or
   margarine
   Chopped fresh parsley for
   garnish

In medium bowl, stir desired soup until smooth; beat in eggs and pepper. In 10-inch skillet over low heat, melt butter. Pour in egg mixture. As eggs begin to set, stir lightly so uncooked egg flows to bottom. Cook until set but still very moist. Garnish with parsley, if desired. Makes 4 servings.

TO MICROWAVE: O*mit* butter or margarine. In 3-quart microwave-safe casserole, stir desired soup until smooth. Beat in eggs and pepper. Cover with lid; microwave on HIGH 6½ minutes or until eggs are nearly set, stirring 3 times during cooking. Let stand, covered, 2 minutes before serving. Garnish with parsley, if desired. Serve immediately.

*Omelet Primavera and Spiced
Sweet Potato Muffins, page 58*

Sea 'n' Shore Puffy Omelet

Here's another serving idea: Spoon the vegetable filling over entire omelet surface and cut into wedges to serve.

1 package (10 ounces) Mrs. Paul's frozen buttered fish fillets	**¼ teaspoon cream of tartar**
½ cup carrots cut into matchstick-thin strips	**1 can (10¾ ounces) Campbell's condensed cream of celery or cream of asparagus soup, divided**
½ cup zucchini cut into matchstick-thin strips	**1 tablespoon butter or margarine**
¼ teaspoon dried basil leaves, crushed	**2 tablespoons milk**
6 eggs, separated	**1 tablespoon lemon juice**

1. Preheat oven to 350°F. In 10-inch skillet over medium heat, cook fish fillets, carrots, zucchini and basil 8 minutes or until fish is done and vegetables are tender, turning fish fillets over once during cooking. Remove from heat.

2. Meanwhile, in large bowl with mixer at high speed, beat egg whites with cream of tartar until stiff peaks form.

3. In small bowl, thoroughly blend egg yolks and *½ cup* of the soup. Gently fold soup mixture into whites.

4. In oven-safe 10-inch skillet over medium heat, melt butter. Pour egg mixture into skillet. Cook about 2 minutes or until underside of omelet is golden.

5. Place skillet in oven; bake 10 minutes or until surface is golden and springs back when pressed *lightly* with fingertips.

6. Meanwhile, with fork, break fillets into coarse pieces. In small bowl, combine remaining soup, milk and lemon juice. Add to fish mixture; stir until blended. Cook over medium heat until heated through.

7. Run spatula around side of skillet to loosen omelet. Spread filling on *half* of omelet. With sharp knife cut down center of omelet, *without cutting through bottom.* With pancake turner, fold omelet in half and slide onto warm platter. Serve immediately. Makes 6 servings.

Country-Style Hash 'n' Eggs

2 tablespoons butter or margarine
4 cups diced cooked potatoes
1 can (10¾ ounces) Campbell's condensed cream of celery soup
¼ cup milk
1 tablespoon Dijon-style mustard

¼ teaspoon hot pepper sauce
1½ cups chopped cooked corned beef or ham
4 eggs
Chopped fresh parsley for garnish

1. In 10-inch skillet over medium heat, in hot butter, cook potatoes 2 minutes, stirring often.

2. Stir in soup, milk, mustard and hot pepper sauce; heat through. Stir in corned beef. Reduce heat to low.

3. Make 4 evenly-spaced indentations in potato mixture. Break 1 egg into each. Cover; cook 10 minutes or until eggs are set. Garnish with parsley, if desired. Makes 4 servings.

Lemon Chicken Omelets

4 tablespoons butter or margarine, divided
2 cups broccoli flowerets
1 clove garlic, minced
1 can (10¾ ounces) Campbell's condensed cream of mushroom, cream of chicken or creamy chicken mushroom soup

1 cup chopped cooked chicken
6 tablespoons water, divided
½ teaspoon grated lemon peel
8 eggs
¼ teaspoon pepper

1. To make chicken filling: In 1½-quart saucepan over medium heat, in *2 tablespoons* hot butter, cook broccoli and garlic until broccoli is tender, stirring occasionally. Stir in soup, chicken, *2 tablespoons* of the water and the lemon peel; heat through. Keep warm.

2. To make omelet: In medium bowl, beat eggs, remaining water and the pepper.

3. In 8-inch nonstick omelet pan or skillet over medium-high heat, melt *½ tablespoon* of the remaining butter. Pour ¼ of the egg mixture (about ½ cup) into pan. Lift edges as eggs set, tilting skillet to allow uncooked egg mixture to flow underneath.

4. When omelet is set but still moist, remove from heat. Spoon *½ cup* of the chicken filling over *half* of omelet. Fold omelet over filling. Slide onto warm plate. Repeat steps 3 and 4 to make 3 more omelets. Makes 4 servings.

Spinach-Potato Scramble

If you use fresh spinach, you'll need about 2 cups loosely-packed leaves. Or, use half of a 10-ounce package frozen chopped spinach. Pictured opposite.

8 ounces Italian sausage,
   casing removed
¼ cup chopped onion
8 eggs
1 can (10¾ ounces) Campbell's
   condensed cream of potato
   soup

½ cup cooked chopped spinach,
   well drained
Sweet red pepper strips and
   celery leaves for garnish

1. In 10-inch skillet over medium heat, cook sausage and onion until sausage is browned and onion is tender, stirring to separate meat. Spoon off fat, reserving *1 tablespoon* of the drippings in skillet. (Add vegetable oil, if necessary.)

2. In medium bowl, beat eggs. Stir in soup and spinach. In same skillet over medium heat, heat sausage and drippings. Pour in egg mixture. As eggs begin to set, stir lightly so uncooked egg flows to bottom. Cook until set but still very moist. Garnish with red pepper and celery leaves, if desired. Makes 6 servings.

TO MICROWAVE: In 3-quart microwave-safe casserole, combine sausage and onion. Cover with lid; microwave on HIGH 3 minutes or until sausage is no longer pink and onion is tender, stirring once during cooking. Spoon off fat, reserving *1 tablespoon* of the drippings in casserole. (Add vegetable oil, if necessary.) In medium bowl, beat eggs. Stir in soup and spinach. Stir egg mixture into sausage and reserved drippings. Cover; microwave on HIGH 8½ minutes or until eggs are nearly set, stirring 4 times during cooking. Let stand, covered, 2 minutes before serving. Garnish as directed in step 2, if desired.

Cheddar Cheese Spoon Bread

1 can (11 ounces) Campbell's
   condensed Cheddar cheese
   soup/sauce
1½ cups milk

¼ cup water
1 cup cornmeal
2 tablespoons butter or margarine
4 eggs

1. Grease 1½-quart casserole. In 3-quart saucepan, stir soup until smooth. Gradually stir in milk and water. Add cornmeal and butter. Over medium heat, heat until mixture boils and thickens, stirring constantly. Remove from heat.

2. In medium bowl with mixer at medium speed, beat eggs until thick and lemon colored. Stir about *1 cup* of the hot soup mixture into eggs; return all to saucepan, stirring constantly. Pour into prepared casserole. Bake at 350°F. for 45 minutes or until knife inserted in center comes out clean. Makes 6 servings.

Spinach-Potato Scramble

Cheesy Baked Grits

2 cans (14½ ounces *each*)
    Swanson clear ready to
    serve chicken broth
1 cup quick-cooking grits,
    uncooked
5 tablespoons butter or
    margarine, divided

½ cup chopped onion
¼ cup chopped sweet red pepper
¼ cup chopped green pepper
1 clove garlic, minced
1½ cups shredded Cheddar cheese
    (6 ounces)
2 eggs, slightly beaten

1. Grease 8- by 8-inch baking dish. In 3-quart saucepan, heat broth to boiling. Slowly add grits, stirring constantly. Cook and stir until boiling. Reduce heat to low; cook 5 minutes or until liquid is absorbed and mixture is thick, stirring constantly.

2. In 8-inch skillet over medium heat, in *2 tablespoons* hot butter, cook onion, red and green peppers and garlic until vegetables are tender, stirring occasionally.

3. Stir cheese, remaining butter and the vegetable mixture into hot grits; stir until butter is melted. Gradually stir about *1 cup* of the hot mixture into eggs; return all to saucepan, stirring constantly.

4. Pour into prepared baking dish. Bake at 325°F. for 35 minutes or until center is nearly set. Let stand 10 minutes. Makes 8 servings.

Spiced Sweet Potato Muffins

These moist-and-spicy muffins are pictured on page 53.

2 cups all-purpose flour
⅓ cup sugar
2 tablespoons baking powder
2 teaspoons ground cinnamon
1 teaspoon ground allspice
1 package (12 ounces) Mrs. Paul's
    frozen candied sweet
    potatoes

¾ cup hot milk
½ cup butter or margarine, melted
2 eggs
½ cup raisins or chopped nuts
    (optional)
Confectioners' sugar (optional)

1. Preheat oven to 375°F. Grease eighteen (2½-inch) muffin cups or line with paper baking cups. In large bowl, stir together flour, sugar, baking powder, cinnamon, allspice and candied sauce mix from sweet potatoes.

2. In covered blender, combine sweet potatoes, milk, butter and eggs. Blend until smooth. Add to flour mixture, stirring just until moistened. Fold in raisins, if desired. (Batter will be very thick.)

3. Fill prepared muffin cups ⅔ full. Bake 15 minutes or until wooden toothpick inserted in center comes out clean. Remove muffins from pans. Sprinkle with confectioners' sugar. Serve warm. Makes 18 muffins.

Ham-and-Egg Pockets

These tasty ham-and-egg sandwiches are delicious to eat for supper, too!

2 tablespoons butter or
   margarine, divided
1½ cups chopped fully cooked ham
¼ cup sliced green onions
8 eggs
1 can (10½ ounces) Franco-
   American golden pork gravy

½ teaspoon prepared mustard
⅛ teaspoon pepper
6 pita breads (6-inch diameter
   sandwich pockets) or long
   hard rolls, halved lengthwise
1 Campbell's Fresh tomato,
   seeded and chopped

1. In 10-inch skillet over medium heat, in *1 tablespoon* hot butter, cook ham and green onions until onions are tender, stirring occasionally.

2. In large bowl, combine eggs, gravy, mustard and pepper; beat until smooth. In same skillet over medium heat, melt remaining butter; pour in egg mixture. As eggs begin to set, stir lightly so uncooked egg flows to bottom. Cook until set but still very moist.

3. Serve in pita bread or split hard rolls; top with tomato. Serve immediately. Makes 6 servings.

TO MICROWAVE: In 3-quart microwave-safe casserole, combine butter, ham and onions. Cover with lid; microwave on HIGH 3 minutes or until onions are tender. In large bowl, combine eggs, gravy, mustard and pepper; beat until smooth. Stir into casserole. Cover; microwave on HIGH 6½ minutes or until eggs are nearly set, stirring 3 times during cooking. Let stand, covered, 2 minutes before serving. Serve as directed in step 3.

Bowl-Time Soups and Sandwiches

Watching football on television with your family and friends is a great excuse for a wintertime party. Choose from this selection of tasty soups and savory sandwiches, such as Jalapeno Chili and zesty White Olive Pizza. Most of the recipes can be prepared ahead so you won't have to miss a minute of the festivities; a few others can be cooked during half-time entertainment.

Beef Stew with Sweet Potatoes

Beef Stew with Sweet Potatoes

While this stew simmers, toss together a colorful garden salad. Serve with French bread and cut-up fruit and cheese. Pictured opposite.

 1 tablespoon vegetable oil
1½ pounds beef for stew, cut into 1-inch pieces
 2 cans (10¾ ounces *each*) Campbell's condensed golden mushroom or beefy mushroom soup
 2 cups water
 1 can (about 8 ounces) tomatoes, undrained, cut up
 1 teaspoon dried marjoram leaves, crushed
 1 package (12 ounces) Mrs. Paul's frozen candied sweet potatoes
 2 cups frozen small whole onions
 2 cups sliced Campbell's Fresh mushrooms

1. In 4-quart Dutch oven over medium heat, in hot oil, cook beef until browned, stirring occasionally.

2. Stir in soup, water, tomatoes with their liquid and marjoram; heat to boiling. Reduce heat to low. Cover; simmer 30 minutes, stirring occasionally.

3. Add sweet potatoes, candied sauce mix, onions and mushrooms; heat to boiling. Reduce heat to low. Cover; simmer 30 minutes more or until vegetables and meat are tender, stirring occasionally. Makes 9 cups or 6 servings.

Jalapeno Chili

When you're expecting a crowd, double the recipe to make a spicy chili that serves eight. Serve with hot corn bread muffins.

½ **pound ground beef**
½ **cup chopped onion**
2 **cans (about 10 ounces** *each***) kidney beans, drained**
1 **can (about 16 ounces) tomatoes, undrained, cut up**
1 **can (10¼ ounces) Franco- American beef gravy**
2 **teaspoons seeded and chopped Vlasic hot jalapeno pepper**
1 **tablespoon chili powder**
1 **teaspoon ground cumin Sour cream Chopped Campbell's Fresh tomatoes Shredded Cheddar cheese**

1. In 10-inch skillet over medium heat, cook beef and onion until beef is browned and onion is tender, stirring to separate meat. Spoon off fat.

2. Stir in beans, tomatoes with their liquid, gravy, jalapeno pepper, chili powder and cumin. Cook over high heat to boiling. Reduce heat to low; simmer, uncovered, 10 minutes.

3. Top individual servings with sour cream, tomatoes and cheese, if desired. Makes 4 cups or 4 servings.

Creamy Chicken-Broccoli Soup

This rich-tasting soup is pretty enough to serve company. Serve with assorted crackers or slices of crusty French bread.

2 **tablespoons butter or margarine**
1 **cup sliced Campbell's Fresh mushrooms**
½ **cup chopped onion**
½ **cup sweet red or green pepper cut into 1-inch strips**
1 **clove garlic, minced**
½ **teaspoon dried basil leaves, crushed**
1 **can (10¾ ounces) Campbell's condensed cream of chicken or cream of broccoli soup**
1 **can (10½ ounces) Campbell's condensed chicken broth**
1¾ **cups milk**
1½ **cups cut-up cooked chicken**
⅛ **teaspoon pepper Generous dash ground nutmeg**
1 **cup broccoli flowerets**

1. In 3-quart saucepan over medium heat, in hot butter, cook mushrooms, onion, red pepper, garlic and basil until vegetables are tender, stirring occasionally.

2. Stir in soup and broth until smooth. Stir in milk, chicken, pepper and nutmeg. Add broccoli; heat to boiling. Reduce heat to low. Cover; simmer 5 minutes or until broccoli is tender. Makes 6 cups or 4 servings.

Sierra Chicken Stew

Serve this colorful stew with warmed tortillas or a basket of crisp corn chips.

1 pound boneless, skinless
    chicken, cut into
    1½-inch pieces
2 tablespoons all-purpose flour
2 tablespoons olive oil
2 cloves garlic, minced
1½ cups water
1 can (11 ounces) Campbell's
    condensed zesty
    tomato soup

1 can (about 8 ounces) whole
    kernel corn with sweet
    peppers, drained
⅓ cup sliced Vlasic pitted ripe
    olives
2 tablespoons lemon juice or
    wine vinegar
Lemon slices and chopped fresh
    parsley for garnish

1. Coat chicken pieces with flour. In 4-quart Dutch oven over medium heat, in hot oil, cook chicken and garlic until chicken is browned, stirring often.

2. Stir in remaining ingredients. Heat to boiling. Reduce heat to low. Simmer, uncovered, 10 minutes or until chicken is tender and juices run clear. Garnish with lemon slices and fresh parsley, if desired. Makes about 5 cups or 4 servings.

Herbed Fish Chowder

For a traditional seafood chowder, garnish soup with oyster crackers.

½ cup water
½ cup chopped carrot
¼ cup chopped celery
¼ cup chopped onion
½ teaspoon dried thyme leaves,
    crushed
1 package (10 ounces) Mrs.
    Paul's frozen buttered
    fish fillets

1¾ cups milk
1 can (10¾ ounces) Campbell's
    condensed cream of potato
    soup
Generous dash pepper

1. In 6-quart Dutch oven over high heat, heat water, carrot, celery, onion and thyme to boiling. Reduce heat to low. Cover; simmer 5 minutes or until vegetables are tender.

2. Add fish; simmer, uncovered, 8 minutes or until fish flakes easily with fork, turning once during cooking. With fork, break fillets into bite-size pieces.

3. Stir in milk, soup and pepper; heat through. Makes 4 cups or 3 servings.

Bountiful Bouillabaisse

After a busy day, this easy, yet elegant, seafood stew will satisfy most appetites. Pictured opposite.

1 can (6½ ounces) chopped clams, undrained
1 tablespoon olive oil
4 cloves garlic, minced
1 can (14½ ounces) Swanson clear ready to serve chicken broth
1 can (about 16 ounces) tomatoes, undrained, cut up
⅓ cup chopped fresh parsley
¼ teaspoon pepper
1 package (10 ounces) Mrs. Paul's frozen buttered fish fillets, cut into quarters
12 ounces medium shrimp, shelled and deveined (about 27)
1 teaspoon orange peel cut into thin strips
Garlic croutons for garnish

1. Drain clams, reserving liquid; set aside.

2. In 3-quart saucepan over medium heat, in hot oil, cook garlic until lightly browned, stirring constantly. Add broth, tomatoes with their liquid, reserved clam liquid, parsley and pepper; heat to boiling. Add fillets; heat to boiling. Reduce heat to low. Simmer, uncovered, 5 minutes.

3. Add clams, shrimp and orange peel. Cook until shrimp are pink and fish flakes easily when tested with fork. Serve with garlic croutons sprinkled on top individual servings, if desired. Makes 6½ cups or 4 servings.

Fish and Caper Croissants

2 packages (9 ounces *each*) Mrs. Paul's frozen prepared light fillets flounder
2 tablespoons Vlasic capers, drained
⅓ cup mayonnaise
2 hard-cooked eggs, chopped
6 large croissants, split and heated
Campbell's Fresh butterhead lettuce leaves
1 Campbell's Fresh tomato, cut into 6 slices

1. Prepare fish according to package directions, reserving both create-a-sauce mix packets.

2. Meanwhile, in small bowl, crush capers with spoon or fork. Add create-a-sauce mix packets, mayonnaise and eggs. Stir to blend.

3. On bottom half of each croissant, arrange lettuce leaves, tomato slice and fish fillet. Evenly spread each fillet with about *2 tablespoons* of the caper sauce. Top with croissant half. Makes 6 sandwiches.

Bountiful Bouillabaisse

Red Sausage Pizza

Frozen bread dough makes this spicy pizza a snap to prepare. Pictured opposite.

1 loaf (1 pound) frozen white
    bread dough, thawed
1 tablespoon olive oil
8 ounces Italian sausage, casing
    removed
1 can (11 ounces) Campbell's
    condensed zesty tomato soup

1 tablespoon vinegar
    Dried oregano leaves
    Cracked pepper
1½ cups shredded mozzarella
    cheese (6 ounces)

1. Preheat oven to 425°F. Grease 15-inch pizza pan or cookie sheet. Roll out or press thawed dough into prepared pan. Brush dough with oil. Bake 12 minutes.

2. Meanwhile, in 10-inch skillet over medium heat, cook sausage until browned, stirring to separate meat. Spoon off fat. Stir in soup and vinegar; heat through.

3. Spread sausage mixture over crust. Sprinkle with oregano and pepper. Top with cheese. Bake 12 minutes or until cheese is melted. Cut into wedges to serve. Makes 4 servings.

Combination Pizza: Prepare as directed in steps 1, 2 and 3 *except* before final baking, add your favorite cut-up toppings, such as onion, green pepper, pepperoni, sliced Vlasic olives or Campbell's Fresh mushrooms.

White Olive Pizza

A quick-to-fix snack for casual gatherings. Try this tomato-less pizza for a change of pace. If you prefer a spicier taste, use the larger amount of red pepper. Pictured opposite.

1 package (10 ounces)
    refrigerated pizza crust
1 tablespoon olive oil
1 cup Vlasic pitted ripe olives
    halved lengthwise
½ teaspoon garlic powder

½ teaspoon dried oregano leaves,
    crushed
¼ to ½ teaspoon crushed red
    pepper
1½ cups shredded mozzarella
    cheese (6 ounces)
¼ cup grated Parmesan cheese

1. Preheat oven to 425°F. Grease 15-inch pizza pan or cookie sheet. Unroll dough; press into prepared pan. Brush dough with oil. Sprinkle with olives, garlic, oregano and red pepper.

2. Bake 15 minutes. Sprinkle cheeses over crust. Bake 5 minutes more or until cheese is melted. Cut into wedges to serve. Makes 4 servings.

White Olive Pizza, Red
Sausage Pizza and Olive Medley
Mediterranean, page 8

Hot Beef and Mushroom Sandwiches

3 tablespoons butter or margarine
1 package (8 ounces) Campbell's
   Fresh mushrooms, sliced
   (3 cups)
¼ cup finely chopped onion
1 can (10¼ ounces) Franco-
   American beef gravy

2 tablespoons ketchup
8 ounces cooked roast beef,
   thinly sliced
6 hard rolls (*each* about 5 inches
   long), split lengthwise

1. In 10-inch skillet over medium heat, in hot butter, cook mushrooms and onion until mushrooms are tender and liquid is evaporated, stirring occasionally.

2. Stir in gravy and ketchup. Heat through, stirring occasionally. Add roast beef. Heat through. Serve on rolls. Makes 6 sandwiches.

Chili Beef Pockets

These portable chili-style sandwiches are easy to eat. And there'll be less cleanup, too.

1 cup cooked or canned red
   kidney beans, drained
1 pound ground beef
1 clove garlic, minced
2 tablespoons chili powder
1 can (10½ ounces) Franco-
   American brown gravy with
   onions

1 can (4 ounces) chopped green
   chilies, drained
1 package (16 ounces) hot
   roll mix
1 egg
1 tablespoon water

1. In small bowl, mash beans with fork; set aside.

2. In 10-inch skillet over medium heat, cook beef, garlic and chili powder until meat is browned, stirring to separate meat. Spoon off fat.

3. Stir in mashed beans, gravy and chilies. Simmer, uncovered, 5 minutes or until thickened, stirring often. Remove from heat; set aside.

4. Preheat oven to 350°F. Grease large cookie sheet. Prepare hot roll dough, then knead and let rest according to package directions. Divide dough into 6 equal portions. On floured surface, roll out each portion to 7-inch round. Spoon about *½ cup* of the beef mixture on dough, spreading to within 1 inch of edges. Fold over to form a half circle. Pinch edges to seal. Repeat with remaining dough and filling. Place 2 inches apart on prepared cookie sheet.

5. In cup, beat egg and water; brush over rolls. Bake 25 minutes or until golden brown. Let cool on wire rack 10 minutes before serving. Makes 6 servings.

Hot and Spicy Tacos

Increase or decrease the amount of jalapeno pepper in the taco filling according to your preference for hotness.

8 taco shells
1 pound lean ground beef
2 cloves garlic, minced
1 tablespoon chili powder
1 can (11 ounces) Campbell's condensed zesty tomato soup
½ cup water

1 tablespoon seeded and chopped Vlasic hot jalapeno pepper
1 tablespoon lime juice
Shredded lettuce
Shredded Cheddar cheese
Sliced Vlasic pitted ripe olives

1. Heat taco shells according to package directions.

2. Meanwhile, in 10-inch skillet over medium heat, cook beef, garlic and chili powder until meat is browned, stirring to separate meat. Spoon off fat.

3. Stir in soup, water, jalapeno pepper and lime juice. Reduce heat to low. Simmer, uncovered, 10 minutes, stirring occasionally.

4. Spoon about *¼ cup* of the beef mixture into each taco shell. Top each with lettuce, cheese and olives. Makes 8 tacos or 4 servings.

Garlic Bread Deluxe

When the gang is really hungry, cut this loaf into 4 meal-sized sandwiches. If you just feel like nibbling, cut into finger-sized portions. Either way, it won't last long!

1 loaf (about 8 ounces) frozen garlic bread
2 cups chopped cooked chicken or turkey
½ cup mayonnaise
1 teaspoon dried basil leaves, crushed

⅓ cup pimento cut into matchstick-thin strips
⅓ cup sliced Vlasic pitted ripe olives
1 tablespoon grated Parmesan cheese

1. Prepare garlic bread according to package directions.

2. Meanwhile, in medium bowl, stir together chicken, mayonnaise and basil.

3. Split garlic bread in half lengthwise. On cookie sheet, place bread cut-side up. Spread each half evenly with chicken mixture; top with pimento, olives and cheese.

4. Broil, 4 inches from heat, 2 to 3 minutes or until bubbling. Cut into 1-inch slices. Makes 4 main-dish or 24 appetizer servings.

Special Side Dishes

Serve any of these dazzling side dishes to round out your holiday menu. Start with attractive Olive-Orange Salad, Creamy Shiitake Soup or a tossed garden salad with one of the piquant salad dressings. Then add a special touch to your entrée with a choice of side dishes, such as festive Red and Green Stir-Fry, Sweet Potato-Stuffed Squash or the all-time favorite Green Bean Bake. All the recipes are suited to easy entertaining and many include timesaving microwave directions, too!

**Harvest Vegetables
with Cheese Sauce**

Harvest Vegetables with Cheese Sauce

Cheese-sauced vegetables are a popular flavor combination and condensed cheese soup makes sauce preparation extra easy. Pictured opposite.

2 packages (10 ounces *each*) frozen Brussels sprouts or 3 cups fresh Brussels sprouts
6 medium carrots, sliced ¼ inch thick (3 cups)
3 cups cauliflowerets
1 can (11 ounces) Campbell's condensed Cheddar cheese soup/sauce
1 package (3 ounces) cream cheese
⅓ cup milk
Generous dash ground red pepper

1. In covered 3-quart saucepan over medium heat, in 1-inch boiling water, cook Brussels sprouts, carrots and cauliflowerets about 10 minutes or until tender, stirring occasionally. Drain in colander.

2. In same pan, combine soup, cream cheese, milk and red pepper. Cook over medium heat until cheese is melted and sauce is smooth, stirring often. Return vegetables to pan; toss gently to coat. Makes 8 cups or 10 servings.

Red and Green Stir-Fry

For easy serving, the cooked rice is mixed in with this colorful vegetable stir-fry. Pictured opposite.

2 tablespoons vegetable oil, divided
2 cups sliced cauliflowerets
1 cup diagonally sliced celery
1 medium onion, coarsely chopped
1 tablespoon grated fresh ginger
1 package (12 ounces) Campbell's Fresh mushrooms, quartered

2 cups snow peas
2 cups coarsely chopped sweet red or green pepper
3 cups hot cooked rice (1 cup uncooked)
1 can (10½ ounces) Franco-American mushroom gravy
1 tablespoon soy sauce

1. In 5-quart Dutch oven or wok over high heat, in *1 tablespoon* hot oil, cook cauliflowerets, celery, onion and ginger, stirring quickly and frequently (stir-frying) until tender-crisp. Transfer to bowl; set aside.

2. In remaining oil, cook mushrooms, peas and red pepper, stirring quickly and frequently until tender-crisp.

3. Add rice, gravy, soy sauce and cooked vegetables; toss gently to mix. Heat through. Makes 9 cups or 12 servings.

Walnut Vegetable Medley

Toss colorful carrots and broccoli with a creamy herb sauce and sprinkle with crunchy walnuts for a company-special side dish.

1 pound carrots, cut into 1½-inch sticks
1 can (10¾ ounces) Campbell's condensed cream of celery or cream of broccoli soup

½ cup milk
1 teaspoon dried basil leaves, crushed
3 cups broccoli flowerets
Toasted chopped walnuts

1. In covered 10-inch skillet over medium heat, in ½-inch boiling water, cook carrots 5 minutes or until tender-crisp. Drain in colander.

2. In same skillet, combine soup, milk and basil until smooth. Add broccoli and cooked carrots. Heat to boiling. Reduce heat to low. Cover; simmer 10 minutes or until vegetables are tender, stirring often. Top with walnuts. Makes 6 cups or 10 servings.

TO MICROWAVE: In 3-quart microwave-safe casserole, add carrots to ½-inch water. Cover with lid; microwave on HIGH 10 minutes or until tender-crisp, stirring once during cooking. Drain in colander; return to casserole. In small bowl, combine soup, milk and basil until smooth. Pour over carrots. Stir in broccoli. Cover; microwave on HIGH 5 minutes or until vegetables are tender, stirring once during cooking. Let stand, covered, 5 minutes. Top with walnuts.

Red and Green Stir-Fry

Green Bean Bake

One of Campbell's most-requested recipes, Green Bean Bake, can be the springboard to other delicious vegetable casseroles. For example, use golden mushroom, cream of celery or cream of chicken soup with asparagus cuts or cauliflowerets.

1 can (10¾ ounces) Campbell's
    condensed cream of
    mushroom soup
½ cup milk
1 teaspoon soy sauce
    Dash pepper

2 packages (9 ounces *each*)
    frozen cut green beans,
    cooked and drained*
1 can (2.8 ounces) French-fried
    onions, divided
¼ cup sliced Vlasic pitted ripe
    olives (optional)

1. In 1½-quart casserole, combine soup, milk, soy sauce and pepper until smooth. Stir in beans, *half* of the onions and the olives.

2. Bake at 350°F. for 25 minutes or until hot; stir. Top with remaining onions. Bake 5 minutes more. Garnish with additional sliced olives, if desired. Makes about 4 cups or 6 servings.

TO MICROWAVE: In 1½-quart microwave-safe casserole, combine soup, milk, soy sauce and pepper until smooth. Stir in green beans, *half* of the onions and the olives. Cover with lid; microwave on HIGH 7 minutes or until hot, stirring once during cooking. Top with remaining onions. Garnish with additional sliced olives, if desired.

*Substitute 2 cans (about 16 ounces *each*) cut green beans (drained) or about 1½ pounds fresh green beans (cooked and drained) for the frozen beans.

Broccoli Bake: Substitute 1 can (10¾ ounces) Campbell's condensed cream of broccoli soup for the cream of mushroom soup. Substitute 2 packages (10 ounces *each*) frozen broccoli spears or cuts, cooked and drained, for the green beans. Omit the ripe olives.

To assemble: In small bowl, combine soup, milk, soy sauce and pepper. In 10- by 6-inch baking dish, layer *half* of the broccoli, ½ cup of the soup mixture and *half* of the onions. Top with remaining broccoli and soup mixture. Bake at 350°F. for 25 minutes. Top with remaining onions. Bake 5 minutes more.

TO MICROWAVE: Assemble as directed above, using a 10- by 6-inch microwave-safe dish. Cover with waxed paper; microwave on HIGH 8 minutes, rotating dish halfway through cooking. Top with remaining onions. Microwave, uncovered, on HIGH 1 minute more.

Sweet Potato-Stuffed Squash

When you can't decide whether to include squash or sweet potatoes in your holiday menu, this tasty recipe allows you to serve both.

2 medium acorn squash (about 1¼ pounds *each*)	¼ cup butter or margarine, melted
2 cups hot water	Generous dash ground cinnamon
1 package (12 ounces) Mrs. Paul's frozen candied sweet potatoes	Generous dash ground nutmeg
	Chopped pecans, walnuts or sliced almonds (optional)

1. Scrub squash. Cut in half lengthwise; remove seeds and stringy fibers.

2. Arrange squash halves, cut-side down, in 13- by 9-inch baking dish. Pour hot water into dish with squash. Bake at 375°F. for 30 minutes; turn squash cut-side up.

3. Divide sweet potatoes among squash cavities. In small bowl, combine candied sauce mix, butter, cinnamon and nutmeg. Divide butter mixture among sweet potatoes. Sprinkle with nuts, if desired.

5. Cover with foil; bake 30 to 35 minutes or until squash and sweet potatoes are fork-tender. Makes 4 servings.

Spirited Sweet Potato Bake

Brandy and nutmeg add a touch of holiday spirit to these scrumptious mashed sweet potatoes.

2 packages (20 ounces *each*) Mrs. Paul's frozen candied sweet potatoes	4 tablespoons butter or margarine, softened, divided
½ cup water	2 tablespoons brandy
	⅛ teaspoon ground nutmeg
	¼ cup chopped pecans

1. Reserve *one* candied sauce mix packet from sweet potatoes. Pour remaining candied sauce mix into 3-quart saucepan. Add water. Heat to boiling, stirring constantly. Add sweet potatoes from *both* packages. Reduce heat to low. Cover; simmer 25 to 30 minutes or until potatoes are tender, stirring occasionally.

2. Preheat oven to 350°F. In medium bowl with mixer at medium speed, mash sweet potatoes while still warm. Add *2 tablespoons* of the butter, the brandy and nutmeg; mix well. Spoon sweet potato mixture into 1½-quart casserole.

3. Meanwhile, combine reserved candied sauce mix, the remaining butter and the pecans; mix until crumbly. Sprinkle over sweet potatoes.

4. Bake, uncovered, 25 minutes or until topping is browned and sweet potatoes are heated through. Makes 4 cups or 8 servings.

Parsnip Sweet Potato Timbales

Sliced baked ham and braised red cabbage compliment the delicate citrus flavor of this elegant vegetable dish. Pictured opposite.

1 package (20 ounces) Mrs. Paul's
   frozen candied sweet
   potatoes
½ cup orange juice
2 tablespoons butter or
   margarine
1 cup peeled and sliced parsnips

1 medium onion, cut into wedges
⅛ teaspoon pepper
   Toasted sliced almonds and
   diced pimento for garnish
4 eggs
1 cup light cream

1. Reserve *2 tablespoons* of the candied sauce mix from sweet potatoes. In 2-quart saucepan, combine remaining sauce mix, orange juice and butter. Over medium heat, heat to boiling. Add sweet potatoes, parsnips, onion and pepper; return to boiling. Reduce heat to low. Cover; simmer 25 minutes or until vegetables are tender, stirring occasionally.

2. Meanwhile, preheat oven to 350°F. Grease eight (6-ounce) custard cups. In bottom of *each* cup, arrange almonds and pimento in decorative pattern, if desired (see photo). Sprinkle reserved candied sauce mix evenly among cups.

3. In covered blender or food processor, blend cooked vegetables and their liquid until smooth. Add eggs and cream; blend until smooth.

4. Divide mixture evenly among custard cups. Place cups in roasting pan. Carefully pour boiling water into pan to reach halfway up sides of cups. Bake 35 minutes or until mixture is puffed and knife inserted in center comes out clean. Remove cups from roasting pan. Cool in cups on wire rack 10 minutes. Invert to serve. Makes 8 servings.

Apples and Sweet Potatoes

This makes a tasty accompaniment to baked ham or roast pork.

1 can (8 ounces) chunk
   pineapple in juice
1 package (20 ounces) Mrs. Paul's
   frozen candied sweet
   potatoes

2 tablespoons butter or margarine
2 tart apples, peeled, cored and
   cut into chunks
¼ teaspoon ground cinnamon

1. Drain pineapple, reserving juice. In 2-quart saucepan, combine pineapple juice, candied sauce mix from sweet potatoes and butter. Over medium heat, heat to boiling. Add sweet potatoes; return to boiling. Reduce heat to low. Cover; simmer 25 minutes or until sweet potatoes are tender, stirring occasionally.

2. Add pineapple, apples and cinnamon; heat through, stirring occasionally. Makes 4 cups or 8 servings.

Parsnip Sweet Potato Timbales

Cranberry-Orange Sweet Potatoes

Serve this flavorful vegetable dish with poultry, ham or pork. The cranberry sauce gives it a festive rosy color.

**2 packages (12 ounces *each*)
   Mrs. Paul's frozen candied
   sweet potatoes
1 cup whole berry cranberry
   sauce**

**1 small orange, sliced, seeded
   and quartered
¼ cup orange juice
2 tablespoons butter or margarine**

1. In 3-quart saucepan, combine candied sauce mix from sweet potatoes, cranberry sauce, orange, orange juice and butter. Over medium heat, heat to boiling, stirring often.

2. Add sweet potatoes; return to boiling. Reduce heat to low. Cover; simmer 25 minutes or until sweet potatoes are tender, stirring occasionally. Makes 3½ cups or 7 servings.

Twice-Baked Potatoes

**3 pounds baking potatoes
   (about 6 large)
   Vegetable oil
¼ cup sour cream
1 can (11 ounces) Campbell's
   condensed Cheddar cheese
   soup/sauce**

**2 tablespoons chopped green
   onion
   Generous dash pepper
   Paprika**

1. Wash and dry potatoes; rub lightly with oil. Prick potatoes with tines of fork. Bake at 400°F. for 1 hour or until potatoes are fork-tender. Remove potatoes from oven.

2. Cut potatoes in half lengthwise. Carefully scoop out pulp from each half, leaving a thin shell.

3. In medium bowl with mixer on medium speed, beat together potato pulp and sour cream. Gradually add soup, green onion and pepper; beat until light and fluffy. Spoon potato mixture into shells. Place on baking sheet. Sprinkle with paprika. Bake 15 minutes until hot. Makes 12 servings.

To assemble ahead: Prepare potatoes as directed through step 3. Arrange in 13- by 9-inch baking dish. Cover; refrigerate up to 6 hours. Sprinkle with paprika. Bake at 350°F. for 35 minutes or until hot.

TO MICROWAVE: *Omit* vegetable oil. Prick potatoes with tines of fork in several places. Arrange potatoes on large microwave-safe plate. Microwave, uncovered, on HIGH 18 minutes or until tender, rearranging potatoes twice during cooking. Continue as directed in steps 2 and 3. Arrange potatoes on large microwave-safe plate. Sprinkle with paprika. Microwave, uncovered, on HIGH 8 minutes or until hot, rotating plate once during heating.

Scalloped Potatoes and Carrots

The potatoes and carrots are very thinly sliced to ensure even cooking in both the conventional and microwave ovens.

1 tablespoon butter or margarine
½ cup chopped onion
¼ teaspoon dried dill weed, crushed
1 can (10½ ounces) Franco-American chicken gravy

1 tablespoon chopped fresh parsley
3 cups peeled and thinly sliced potatoes
½ cup very thinly sliced carrot

1. Grease 1-quart casserole. In 1-quart saucepan over medium heat, in hot butter, cook onion and dill until onion is tender, stirring occasionally.

2. Stir in gravy and parsley. Heat through. Remove from heat.

3. In prepared casserole, layer *half* of the potatoes and carrot. Spoon *half* of the gravy mixture over vegetables. Repeat layers.

4. Cover; bake at 425°F. for 30 minutes. Uncover; bake 15 minutes more or until potatoes and carrots are tender. Let stand 5 minutes before serving. Makes 4 servings.

TO MICROWAVE: *Omit* butter. In 1½-quart microwave-safe casserole, stir together onion, dill, gravy and parsley. Cover with lid; microwave on HIGH 4 minutes or until onion is tender, stirring once during cooking. Stir in potatoes and carrot. Cover; microwave on HIGH 12 minutes or until potatoes and carrots are tender, stirring twice during cooking. Let stand, covered, 5 minutes before serving.

Spiced Cranberry-Nut Stuffing

½ cup butter or margarine
2 cups sliced celery
1 package (16 ounces) herb seasoned stuffing mix
1 can (14½ ounces) Swanson clear ready to serve chicken broth

1 cup whole berry cranberry sauce
½ cup coarsely chopped toasted nuts
1 egg, beaten
1 teaspoon grated orange peel
¼ teaspoon ground cinnamon

1. Grease 2-quart casserole. In 4-quart saucepan over medium heat, in hot butter, cook celery until tender. Add remaining ingredients; toss to mix well.

2. Spoon into prepared casserole. Cover; bake at 375°F. for 30 minutes or until hot. Makes 8 cups or 16 servings.

NOTE: Stuffing can be prepared as directed in step 1 and used to stuff a 14- to 16-pound turkey.

Broccoli and Wild Rice Pilaf

To save you time, assemble this crowd-pleasing rice bake in advance. Just cover and refrigerate up to 24 hours before baking. Add 10 minutes to the baking time. Pictured opposite.

2 cans (14½ ounces *each*) Swanson clear ready to serve chicken broth
¾ cup wild rice, uncooked
1 cup regular long-grain rice, uncooked
½ cup butter or margarine
1 cup chopped onions

2 carrots, halved lengthwise and sliced
1 clove garlic, minced
½ teaspoon dried rosemary leaves, crushed
1 package (10 ounces) frozen broccoli spears, thawed and coarsely chopped
¼ teaspoon pepper

1. In 3-quart saucepan over high heat, heat broth to boiling. Add wild rice. Reduce heat to low. Cover; simmer 25 minutes. Add long-grain rice. Cover; simmer 20 minutes or until liquid is absorbed. Remove from heat.

2. Grease 2-quart casserole. Meanwhile, in 4-quart saucepan over medium heat, in hot butter, cook onions, carrots, garlic and rosemary about 10 minutes or until carrots are tender-crisp, stirring occasionally.

3. Add cooked rice, broccoli and pepper to mixture; toss gently to mix well. Spoon into prepared casserole. Cover; bake at 375°F. for 30 minutes or until hot. Stir before serving to fluff. Makes 7½ cups or 10 servings.

Carrot-Mushroom Pilaf

This savory rice pilaf is a delicious accompaniment to fish or poultry entrées.

3 slices bacon
1 cup sliced Campbell's Fresh mushrooms
½ cup diagonally sliced celery
¼ cup sliced green onions

½ cup regular long-grain rice, uncooked
1 can (10½ ounces) Franco-American au jus gravy
¼ cup shredded carrot
¼ teaspoon poultry seasoning

1. In 10-inch skillet over medium heat, cook bacon until crisp. Transfer to paper towel to drain; crumble. Reserve *2 tablespoons* of the drippings in skillet; discard remaining.

2. In drippings in skillet, cook mushrooms, celery and green onions until celery is tender-crisp, stirring occasionally. Add rice; stir to coat. Add gravy, carrot and poultry seasoning. Reduce heat to low. Cover; simmer 25 minutes or until all liquid is absorbed and rice is tender, stirring occasionally. Makes about 2 cups or 4 servings.

Broccoli and Wild Rice Pilaf

Creamy Shiitake Soup

The sophisticated flavors in this mushroom soup are sure to please your holiday dinner guests.

1 package (3.5 ounces) Campbell's Fresh shiitake mushrooms
2 tablespoons butter or margarine
1 package (8 ounces) Campbell's Fresh mushrooms, sliced
¼ cup sliced green onions

1 tablespoon all-purpose flour
1 can (14½ ounces) Swanson clear ready to serve beef broth
1 cup light cream
Freshly ground pepper

1. Trim woody portion of shiitake mushroom stems. Remove and chop stems; slice mushroom caps.

2. In 2-quart saucepan over medium heat, in hot butter, cook shiitake stems briefly to soften. Add sliced shiitake caps, sliced mushrooms and green onions; cook until tender, stirring occasionally. Add flour, stirring until well blended.

3. Stir in broth and cream; heat through. Sprinkle with pepper. Makes 4 cups or 4 servings.

Creamy Fresh Broccoli Soup

Serve as a first-course soup at your next dinner party.

1 pound fresh broccoli, cut into 1-inch pieces
3 tablespoons butter or margarine
⅓ cup chopped onion
¼ teaspoon ground nutmeg
3 tablespoons all-purpose flour

1 can (14½ ounces) Swanson clear ready to serve chicken broth
1 cup milk
Lemon slices for garnish

1. In covered 3-quart saucepan in 1-inch boiling water, cook broccoli 5 minutes or until tender. Drain in colander.

2. In same saucepan over medium heat, in hot butter, cook onion and nutmeg until onion is tender, stirring occasionally. Stir in flour; cook 1 minute, stirring constantly. Gradually stir in broth; cook until mixture boils and thickens, stirring constantly.

3. Add milk and broccoli, heat through, stirring occasionally. Garnish with lemon slices, if desired. Makes 4½ cups or 4 servings.

Herbed Tortellini Soup

2 cans (14½ ounces *each*)
  Swanson clear ready to
  serve chicken broth
1 can (about 16 ounces) tomatoes,
  drained, cut up
1 can (about 16 ounces) chick
  peas, rinsed and drained
2 cloves garlic, minced

1 teaspoon dried basil leaves,
  crushed
2 cups fresh or frozen cheese
  tortellini, cooked and
  drained
2 tablespoons chopped fresh
  parsley
Grated Parmesan cheese

1. In 3-quart saucepan over medium heat, heat broth, tomatoes, chick peas, garlic and basil to boiling. Reduce heat to low.

2. Add tortellini. Heat through, stirring occasionally. Stir in parsley before serving. Serve with Parmesan. Makes about 7 cups or 6 servings.

Carrot-Sweet Potato Soup

This creamy vegetable soup, flecked with carrots and pecans, is delicious served with a wedge of freshly-baked quiche and fresh fruit.

2 cups chopped carrots
1 can (14½ ounces) Swanson
  clear ready to serve chicken
  broth
1 package (12 ounces) Mrs. Paul's
  frozen candied sweet
  potatoes

1¼ cups milk
⅛ teaspoon ground nutmeg
  Chopped toasted pecans for
  garnish

1. In 2-quart saucepan, combine carrots, broth, sweet potatoes and candied sauce mix. Over high heat, heat to boiling. Reduce heat to low. Cover; simmer 20 minutes or until vegetables are tender.

2. With slotted spoon, remove ½ cup of the carrots; reserve. In covered blender or food processor, combine cooked vegetable mixture, milk and nutmeg. Blend until smooth.

3. Return puréed mixture and reserved carrots to saucepan; heat through. Thin with additional milk to desired consistency. Garnish with toasted pecans, if desired. Makes 4 cups or 4 servings.

TO MICROWAVE: In 2-quart microwave-safe casserole, combine sweet potatoes and carrots. Pour candied sauce mix *evenly* over vegetables. Add ¼ cup of the chicken broth. Cover with lid; microwave on HIGH 15 minutes or until vegetables are tender, stirring once during cooking. Stir in remaining broth. Proceed as directed in step 2. Return puréed mixture and reserved carrots to casserole. Cover; microwave on HIGH 6 minutes or until heated through, stirring once during cooking. Serve as directed in step 3.

Olive-Orange Salad

A refreshing and colorful combination — perfect to begin a holiday meal or serve at a buffet. Pictured opposite.

6 large oranges, peeled, sliced
    and seeded
¾ cup Vlasic pitted ripe olives
    halved lengthwise
1 large red onion, sliced and
    separated into rings

¼ cup orange juice
¼ cup olive oil
⅛ teaspoon ground red pepper
    Campbell's Fresh butterhead
    lettuce leaves for garnish

1. In large bowl, combine oranges, olives, onion, orange juice, oil and red pepper; toss gently to coat. Cover; refrigerate at least 2 hours before serving.

2. To serve: Arrange chilled fruit mixture on lettuce-lined platter. Makes 6 cups or 6 servings.

Dijon-Parmesan Dressing

1 can (14½ ounces) Swanson
    clear ready to serve chicken
    broth
1 package (8 ounces) cream
    cheese

½ cup grated Parmesan cheese
3 tablespoons Dijon-style
    mustard
2 tablespoons vinegar
1 clove garlic, minced

In covered blender or food processor, combine all ingredients. Blend until smooth. Refrigerate at least 2 hours before serving. Serve over torn salad greens. Makes 3⅓ cups.

Chili Dressing

Spoon Chili Dressing over a platter of avocado, tomato and green onion slices for a festive salad.

1 can (14½ ounces) Swanson
    clear ready to serve chicken
    broth
1 can (6 ounces) tomato paste
1 tablespoon vegetable oil
1 tablespoon vinegar

1 tablespoon Louisiana-style hot
    sauce
1 tablespoon honey
1 clove garlic, minced
⅛ teaspoon onion powder
    Generous dash pepper

In medium bowl, combine all ingredients until smooth. Cover; refrigerate at least 2 hours before serving. Shake well before using. Serve over torn salad greens. Makes 2½ cups.

Olive-Orange Salad

Festive Desserts

This chapter is bursting with treats designed to satisfy most every sweet tooth. Choose from chewy Old-Fashioned Applesauce Oatmeal Cookies, rich-and-creamy Sweet Potato Cheesecake, Chocolate-Cherry Pound Cake and more! These dessert specialties will end your holiday meal on a festive note, deliciously!

Top: Chocolate-Cherry Pound Cake, page 90
Bottom: Christmas Pound Cake

Christmas Pound Cake

This fruit-studded cake is a tasty choice for those who like pound cake, but aren't fond of traditional fruitcake. Pictured opposite.

2 jars (6 ounces *each*) Vlasic red or green maraschino cherries, drained and chopped (1 cup)
1 cup chopped candied pineapple
1 cup chopped almonds
1 cup flaked coconut
1 cup golden raisins
⅓ cup candied citron
1 package (16 ounces) pound cake mix
1 can (11 ounces) Campbell's condensed Cheddar cheese soup/sauce
3 eggs
1 teaspoon vanilla extract

1. Preheat oven to 325°F. Grease two 8½- by 4½-inch loaf pans.

2. In medium bowl, combine cherries, pineapple, almonds, coconut, raisins and citron. Set aside.

3. In large bowl with mixer at medium speed, beat cake mix, soup, eggs and vanilla 2 minutes, scraping bowl occasionally. Stir in fruit mixture. Pour batter into prepared pans.

4. Bake 1 hour 10 minutes or until wooden toothpick inserted in center comes out clean. Let stand in pans on wire rack 10 minutes. Remove from pans; cool completely. Wrap in foil. Refrigerate 12 hours for easier slicing. Makes 2 loaves.

VARIATION: Preheat oven to 325°F. Grease five 6- by 3-inch loaf pans. Prepare batter as directed in steps 2 and 3. Pour into prepared loaf pans. Bake 55 to 60 minutes or until wooden toothpick inserted in center comes out clean. Cool and wrap as directed in step 4.

Christmas Stollen

This pretty braid is pictured opposite and on back cover.

1 cup candied citrus peel
1 cup raisins
½ cup coarsely chopped Vlasic red or green maraschino cherries
½ cup light rum
1 can (11 ounces) Campbell's condensed Cheddar cheese soup/sauce
1 cup milk
1 cup butter or margarine

8½ to 9 cups all-purpose flour
1 cup sugar
2 packages active dry yeast
½ teaspoon grated lemon peel
2 eggs
½ teaspoon almond extract
½ cup sliced almonds
2 tablespoons butter or margarine, melted
Confectioners' sugar

1. In medium bowl, combine candied peel, raisins, cherries and rum. Let stand 1 hour. Drain fruit, reserving rum. Grease 2 large cookie sheets.

2. In 2-quart saucepan, combine soup and milk. Add the 1 cup butter and reserved rum. Over medium heat, heat until very warm (120° to 130°F.).

3. In large bowl with mixer at low speed, beat *3 cups* of the flour, the sugar, yeast and lemon peel until blended. Add warm soup mixture; beat at medium speed 2 minutes, scraping bowl. Add *2 cups* of the flour, the eggs and extract. Beat at medium speed 2 minutes, scraping bowl occasionally.

4. Stir in almonds, prepared fruit mixture and enough remaining flour to make a stiff dough. On lightly floured surface, knead dough about 10 minutes until smooth and elastic, adding flour as necessary. Place in greased large bowl; turn to coat.

5. Cover with towel; let rise in warm place 1 to 1½ hours or until doubled in size. Punch down dough.

6. To shape loaves: Divide dough in half; set aside *one* half while shaping the first loaf. For *each* loaf, divide each half into 2 parts, one about ⅔ of the dough and the other about ⅓ of the dough. Divide larger part into 3 equal pieces. Roll each piece into a 12-inch-long rope. On prepared cookie sheet, press the ropes together at one end; braid ropes. Pinch other end of ropes together; fold ends under. Divide smaller part into 3 equal pieces. Roll each piece into a 10-inch-long rope. Press ropes together at one end; braid ropes. Pinch other ends of ropes together; fold ends under. Center small braid on top the large braid. Pinch braids together at ends to seal.

7. Repeat with remaining dough to form second loaf. Cover; let rise in warm place about 45 minutes or until doubled in size. Preheat oven to 375°F. Brush loaves with melted butter.

8. Bake 15 minutes. Cover loosely with foil; bake 15 minutes more or until loaves sound hollow when tapped. Remove from cookie sheets. Let stand on wire racks 1 hour. Sprinkle with confectioners' sugar. Makes 2 loaves.

Christmas Stollen

Chocolate-Cherry Pound Cake

A delicious addition to any dessert table. Pictured on page 86.

3 cups all-purpose flour
2 teaspoons baking powder
½ teaspoon baking soda
1 cup chopped Vlasic red and
   green maraschino cherries
1 cup semi-sweet chocolate
   pieces
1 cup chopped dates
1 cup chopped walnuts
1 cup sugar

½ cup butter or margarine
3 eggs
1¼ cups milk
¼ cup creme de cassis or
   cherry-flavored brandy
½ cup confectioners' sugar
2 to 3 teaspoons water or milk
Vlasic red and green
   maraschino cherries for
   garnish

1. Preheat oven to 350°F. Grease 10-inch Bundt® pan. In medium bowl, stir together flour, baking powder and baking soda. Add cherries, chocolate pieces, dates and walnuts; toss to coat.

2. In large bowl with mixer at medium speed, beat sugar and butter about 2 minutes or until light and fluffy. Add eggs, one at a time, beating until smooth and scraping bowl occasionally. Add milk and liqueur; beat until mixed. Add flour mixture; stir until mixed. Pour batter into prepared pan.

3. Bake 55 minutes or until wooden toothpick inserted in center comes out clean. Let stand on wire rack 10 minutes. Remove from pan; cool completely.

4. For glaze, in small bowl, stir together confectioners' sugar and *2 teaspoons* of the water. If necessary, add more water. Drizzle glaze over cake. Garnish with cherries, if desired. Makes 16 servings.

Old-Fashioned Applesauce Oatmeal Cookies

2 cups all-purpose flour
1 tablespoon ground cinnamon
1½ teaspoons baking powder
½ teaspoon baking soda
1 can (11 ounces) Campbell's
   condensed Cheddar cheese
   soup/sauce
1½ cups packed brown sugar

1 cup applesauce
1 cup shortening
2 eggs
2 cups quick-cooking oats
1 cup raisins
1 cup chopped nuts (walnuts,
   pecans or peanuts)

1. Preheat oven to 350°F. In large bowl, stir together flour, cinnamon, baking powder and baking soda.

2. Add soup, sugar, applesauce, shortening and eggs. With mixer at medium speed, beat 2 minutes, scraping bowl. Stir in oats, raisins and nuts.

3. Drop dough by rounded teaspoonfuls, 2 inches apart, onto cookie sheet. Bake 15 minutes or until golden. Remove from cookie sheet. Makes 7½ dozen cookies.

Tomato Spice Cake

Bake this versatile spice cake for any occasion — as a sheet cake, in layers, cupcakes or as a Bundt® cake. Frost with cream cheese frosting and sprinkle with broken walnuts or pecans.

2 cups all-purpose flour
1⅓ cups sugar
4 teaspoons baking powder
1½ teaspoons ground allspice
1 teaspoon baking soda
1 teaspoon ground cinnamon
½ teaspoon ground cloves
**1 can (10¾ ounces) Campbell's
    condensed tomato soup**
½ cup shortening
2 eggs
¼ cup water

1. Preheat oven to 350°F. Grease and flour 13- by 9-inch baking pan.

2. In large bowl, combine all ingredients. With mixer at low speed, beat until well mixed, scraping bowl constantly. At high speed, beat 4 minutes, scraping bowl occasionally. Pour into prepared pan.

3. Bake 40 minutes or until wooden toothpick inserted in center comes out clean. Let stand in pan on wire rack, cool completely. Frost as desired. Makes 12 servings.

Tomato Soup Layer Cake: Preheat oven to 350°F. Grease and flour two (8-inch) round cake pans. Prepare batter as directed in step 2; pour into prepared pans. Bake 35 to 40 minutes. Let stand in pans on wire rack 10 minutes. Remove from pans; cool completely. Frost.

Cupcakes: Preheat oven to 350°F. Place paper liners in twenty-four (3-inch) muffin cups or grease and flour cups. Prepare batter as directed in step 2; spoon into cups, filling ½ full. Bake 30 minutes. Cool as directed in step 3.

Tomato Soup Bundt® Cake: Preheat oven to 350°F. Grease and flour 10-inch Bundt® pan. Prepare batter as directed in step 2; pour into prepared pan. Bake 1 hour. Let stand in pan on wire rack 10 minutes. Remove from pan; cool completely. Sprinkle with confectioners' sugar.

Quick Tomato Spice Cake: Substitute 1 package (about 18 ounces) spice cake mix for dry ingredients and shortening. Increase water to ½ *cup*. Mix and bake according to package directions. Cool as directed in step 3.

Sweet Potato Cheesecake

This elegant-looking cheesecake is easy to decorate. Pictured opposite.

1 package (12 ounces) Mrs. Paul's frozen candied sweet potatoes
1½ cups light cream
2 cups graham cracker crumbs (about 22 crackers)
⅓ cup butter or margarine, melted
½ cup sugar, divided

3 packages (8 ounces *each*) cream cheese, softened
1 teaspoon vanilla extract
4 eggs
½ teaspoon grated orange peel
Whipped cream, mint leaves, candied violets, cranberries, orange peel and sugared rose petals for garnish

1. Prepare sweet potatoes according to package directions; cool slightly. Preheat oven to 325°F. In covered blender or food processor, combine cooked sweet potatoes and cream. Set aside.

2. In small bowl, combine crumbs, butter and ¼ *cup* of the sugar. Press mixture firmly onto bottom and 2 inches up side of 9-inch springform pan.

3. In large bowl with mixer at medium speed, beat cream cheese, vanilla and remaining sugar until light and fluffy. Add eggs, one at a time, beating until smooth, scraping bowl. Add puréed sweet potato mixture and orange peel; beat until smooth. Pour into crumb crust; place on jelly-roll pan.

4. Bake 60 to 70 minutes or until center is just set. Cool on wire rack. Cover; refrigerate at least 8 hours. Garnish with the garnishes suggested above. Makes 16 servings.

TIP: To make sugared rose petals, brush pesticide-free rose petals with lightly beaten egg white and sprinkle with granulated sugar. Let dry on wire racks for a few hours. Store in airtight containers.

Spiced Sweet Potato Pie

1 package (20 ounces) Mrs. Paul's frozen candied sweet potatoes
⅓ cup sugar
1 teaspoon ground cinnamon
1 teaspoon vanilla extract

½ teaspoon ground ginger
¼ teaspoon ground nutmeg
1 cup milk
3 eggs
9-inch unbaked piecrust
Sweetened whipped cream

1. Prepare sweet potatoes according to package directions; cool slightly. Preheat oven to 375°F. In covered blender or food processor, combine potatoes, sugar, cinnamon, vanilla, ginger and nutmeg. Blend well. Add milk and eggs. Blend until well mixed. Pour into piecrust.

2. Bake 45 minutes or until knife inserted off center comes out clean. (Pie will be puffy and sink as it cools.) Cool. Serve with whipped cream. Makes 8 servings.

Sweet Potato Cheesecake

Index

Appetizers
 Basil-Mushroom Dip, 19
 Broiled Shrimp Dijon, 15
 Crab Parmesan Toasts, 14
 Crab with Caper-Dill Dip, 7
 Feta-Olive Turnovers, 18
 Fresh Vegetable Marinade, 8
 Gingered Turkey Meatballs, 10
 Herb Cheesecake, 12
 Hot and Spicy Chicken Wings, 11
 Lime-Ginger Skewered Chicken, 11
 Mushroom Crescents, 16
 Nachos Olé!, 14
 Olive Medley Mediterranean, 8
 Olive-Stuffed Cheese Balls, 18
 Pecan-Olive Canapes, 19
 Spicy Meatballs, 10
 Stuffed Mushrooms Florentine, 15
 Tomato-Olive Salsa, 19
Apples and Sweet Potatoes, 76
Artichoke-Stuffed Chicken Breasts, 32

Basil-Mushroom Dip, 19
Beef (*see also* **Ground Beef**)
 Beef Paprikash with Noodles, 39
 Beef Scallops in Burgundy Sauce, 22
 Beef Stew with Sweet Potatoes, 61
 Country-Style Hash 'n' Eggs, 55
 Ginger Beef Stir-Fry, 21
 Hot Beef and Mushroom Sandwiches, 68
 Roast Beef with Dijon Gravy, 22
 Vegetable-Stuffed Flank Steak, 24
Bountiful Bouillabaisse, 64
Breads
 Cheddar Cheese Spoon Bread, 56
 Christmas Stollen, 88
 Spiced Sweet Potato Muffins, 58
Broccoli and Wild Rice Pilaf, 80
Broccoli Bake, 74
Broiled Shrimp Dijon, 15
Buttermilk Chicken Gravy, 36

Cakes (*see also* **Desserts**)
Campbelled Eggs, 52
Caper Turkey Salad Sandwiches, 45
Caraway Turkey-Noodle Bake, 42
Carrots
 Carrot-Mushroom Pilaf, 80
 Carrot-Sweet Potato Soup, 83
 Scalloped Potatoes and Carrots, 79
Cheddar Cheese Spoon Bread, 56

Cheese
 Cheddar Cheese Spoon Bread, 56
 Cheesy Baked Grits, 58
 Combination Pizza, 66
 Crab Parmesan Toasts, 14
 Dijon-Parmesan Dressing, 84
 Feta-Olive Turnovers, 18
 Harvest Vegetables with Cheese Sauce, 71
 Herb Cheesecake, 12
 Mushroom Quiche, 49
 Nacho Broccoli Strata, 51
 Olive-Stuffed Cheese Balls, 18
 Pecan-Olive Canapes, 19
 Red Sausage Pizza, 66
 Sweet Potato Cheesecake, 92
 Turkey-and-Stuffing au Gratin, 40
 Two-Cheese Soufflé, 51
 White Olive Pizza, 66
Cheesy Baked Grits, 58
Chicken (*see also* **Turkey**)
 Artichoke-Stuffed Chicken Breasts, 32
 Chicken Broccoli Pasta Parmesan, 29
 Creamy Chicken-Broccoli Soup, 62
 Garlic Bread Deluxe, 69
 Hot and Spicy Chicken Wings, 11
 Lemon Chicken Omelets, 55
 Lime-Ginger Skewered Chicken, 11
 Sierra Chicken Stew, 63
 Spicy Chicken and Vegetables, 29
Chili Beef Pockets, 68
Chili Dressing, 84
Chocolate-Cherry Pound Cake, 90
Christmas Pound Cake, 87
Christmas Stollen, 88
Combination Pizza, 66
Cookies, Old-Fashioned Applesauce Oatmeal, 90
Country-Style Hash 'n' Eggs, 55
Crab Parmesan Toasts, 14
Crab with Caper-Dill Dip, 7
Cranberry-Orange Sweet Potatoes, 78
Creamy Chicken-Broccoli Soup, 62
Creamy Fresh Broccoli Soup, 82
Creamy Shiitake Soup, 82

Desserts
 Chocolate-Cherry Pound Cake, 90
 Christmas Pound Cake, 87
 Christmas Stollen, 88
 Old-Fashioned Applesauce Oatmeal
  Cookies, 90
 Spiced Sweet Potato Pie, 92

Sweet Potato Cheesecake, 92
Tomato Spice Cake, 91
Dijon-Parmesan Dressing, 84

Eggs
Campbelled Eggs, 52
Cheesy Baked Grits, 58
Country-Style Hash 'n' Eggs, 55
Ham-and-Egg Pockets, 59
Lemon Chicken Omelets, 55
Mushroom Quiche, 49
Nacho Broccoli Strata, 51
Omelet Primavera, 52
Parsnip Sweet Potato Timbales, 76
Potato-Egg Pie, 50
Sea 'n' Shore Puffy Omelet, 54
Spinach-Potato Scramble, 56
Tortilla Egg Bake, 50
Two-Cheese Soufflé, 51

Feta-Olive Turnovers, 18
Fish and Shellfish
Bountiful Bouillabaisse, 64
Broiled Shrimp Dijon, 15
Crab Parmesan Toasts, 14
Crab with Caper-Dill Dip, 7
Fish and Caper Croissants, 64
Fish with Caper Salsa, 36
Fish with Tangy Mustard Sauce, 34
Herbed Fish Chowder, 63
Lemon Garlic Shrimp, 34
Sea 'n' Shore Puffy Omelet, 54
Fresh Vegetable Marinade, 8

Garden Vegetable Gravy, 37
Garlic Bread Deluxe, 69
Ginger Beef Stir-Fry, 21
Gingered Turkey Meatballs, 10
Ginger-Turkey Spaghetti, 44
Gravies and Sauces
Buttermilk Chicken Gravy, 36
Fish with Caper Salsa, 36
Garden Vegetable Gravy, 37
Shiitake Wine Sauce, 37
Tomato-Olive Salsa, 19
Turkey Gravy Dijon, 36
Green Bean Bake, 74
Grits, Cheesy Baked, 58
Ground Beef (*see also* **Beef**)
Chili Beef Pockets, 68
Hot and Spicy Tacos, 69
Jalapeno Chili, 62
Spicy Meatballs, 10

Ham
Ham-and-Egg Pockets, 59
Ham with Cornmeal Biscuits, 46
Mushroom-Stuffed Ham, 28
Pineapple-Glazed Ham and Sweet Potatoes, 28
Red Beans and Rice, 45
Tortellini with Mushrooms and Ham, 46
Harvest Vegetables with Cheese Sauce, 71
Herb Cheesecake, 12
Herbed Fish Chowder, 63
Herbed Tortellini Soup, 83

Herb-Stuffed Turkey, 30
Hot and Spicy Chicken Wings, 11
Hot and Spicy Tacos, 69
Hot Beef and Mushroom Sandwiches, 68

Jalapeno Chili, 62

Lemon Chicken Omelets, 55
Lemon Garlic Shrimp, 34
Lime-Ginger Skewered Chicken, 11

Mediterranean-Style Fettuccine, 42
Microwave Recipes
Artichoke-Stuffed Chicken Breasts, 32
Broccoli Bake, 74
Campbelled Eggs, 52
Caraway Turkey-Noodle Bake, 42
Carrot-Sweet Potato Soup, 83
Garden Vegetable Gravy, 37
Green Bean Bake, 74
Ham-and-Egg Pockets, 59
Lemon Garlic Shrimp, 34
Nachos Olé!, 14
Pineapple-Glazed Ham and Sweet Potatoes, 28
Scalloped Potatoes and Carrots, 79
Spinach-Potato Scramble, 56
Turkey-and-Stuffing au Gratin, 40
Turkey-Broccoli Divan, 41
Turkey Gravy Dijon, 36
Twice-Baked Potatoes, 78
Walnut Vegetable Medley, 72
Mushrooms
Basil-Mushroom Dip, 19
Carrot-Mushroom Pilaf, 80
Creamy Shiitake Soup, 82
Fresh Vegetable Marinade, 8
Hot Beef and Mushroom Sandwiches, 68
Mushroom Crescents, 16
Mushroom Quiche, 49
Mushroom-Stuffed Ham, 28
Red and Green Stir-Fry, 72
Shiitake Wine Sauce, 37
Stuffed Mushrooms Florentine, 15

Nacho Broccoli Strata, 51
Nachos Olé!, 14
Nacho Turkey Puff, 40

Old-Fashioned Applesauce Oatmeal Cookies, 90
Olive Medley Mediterranean, 8
Olive-Orange Salad, 84
Olive-Stuffed Cheese Balls, 18
Omelet Primavera, 52

Parsnip Sweet Potato Timbales, 76
Pecan-Olive Canapes, 19
Pesto-Stuffed Veal Roast, 23
Pineapple-Glazed Ham and Sweet Potatoes, 28
Piquant Pork Chops, 26
Pork
Piquant Pork Chops, 26
Spiced Pork Loin with Sweet Potatoes, 26
Potatoes
Country-Style Hash 'n' Eggs, 55
Potato-Egg Pie, 50
continued

continued
    Scalloped Potatoes and Carrots, 79
    Twice-Baked Potatoes, 78

Red and Green Stir-Fry, 72
Red Beans and Rice, 45
Red Sausage Pizza, 66
Rice
    Broccoli and Wild Rice Pilaf, 80
    Carrot-Mushroom Pilaf, 80
    Red and Green Stir-Fry, 72
    Red Beans and Rice, 45
Roast Beef with Dijon Gravy, 22

Salads and Dressings
    Chili Dressing, 84
    Dijon-Parmesan Dressing, 84
    Fresh Vegetable Marinade, 8
    Olive Medley Mediterranean, 8
    Olive-Orange Salad, 84
Sausage
    Combination Pizza, 66
    Red Sausage Pizza, 66
    Spicy Chicken and Vegetables, 29
    Spicy Meatballs, 10
    Spinach-Potato Scramble, 56
Scalloped Potatoes and Carrots, 79
Sea 'n' Shore Puffy Omelet, 54
Shiitake Wine Sauce, 37
Sierra Chicken Stew, 63
Soufflé, Two-Cheese, 51
Soups and Stews
    Beef Stew with Sweet Potatoes, 61
    Bountiful Bouillabaisse, 64
    Carrot-Sweet Potato Soup, 83
    Creamy Chicken-Broccoli Soup, 62
    Creamy Fresh Broccoli Soup, 82
    Creamy Shiitake Soup, 82
    Herbed Fish Chowder, 63
    Herbed Tortellini Soup, 83
    Jalapeno Chili, 62
    Sierra Chicken Stew, 63
Spiced Cranberry-Nut Stuffing, 79
Spiced Pork Loin with Sweet Potatoes, 26
Spiced Sweet Potato Muffins, 58
Spiced Sweet Potato Pie, 92
Spicy Chicken and Vegetables, 29
Spicy Meatballs, 10
Spinach-Potato Scramble, 56
Spirited Sweet Potato Bake, 75
Stuffed Mushrooms Florentine, 15
Stuffing, Spiced Cranberry-Nut, 79
Sweet Potatoes
    Apples and Sweet Potatoes, 76
    Beef Stew with Sweet Potatoes, 61
    Carrot-Sweet Potato Soup, 83
    Cranberry-Orange Sweet Potatoes, 78
    Parsnip Sweet Potato Timbales, 76
    Spiced Pork Loin with Sweet Potatoes, 26
    Spiced Sweet Potato Muffins, 58
    Spiced Sweet Potato Pie, 92
    Spicy Chicken and Vegetables, 29
    Spirited Sweet Potato Bake, 75
    Sweet Potato Cheesecake, 92

Sweet Potato Shepherd's Pie, 41
Sweet Potato-Stuffed Squash, 75

Tomato-Olive Salsa, 19
Tomato Spice Cake, 91
Tortellini with Mushrooms and Ham, 46
Tortilla Egg Bake, 50
Turkey (*see also* **Chicken**)
    Caper Turkey Salad Sandwiches, 45
    Caraway Turkey-Noodle Bake, 42
    Gingered Turkey Meatballs, 10
    Ginger-Turkey Spaghetti, 44
    Herb-Stuffed Turkey, 30
    Mediterranean-Style Fettuccine, 42
    Nacho Turkey Puff, 40
    Sweet Potato Shepherd's Pie, 41
    Turkey and Dumplings, 44
    Turkey-and-Stuffing au Gratin, 40
    Turkey-Broccoli Divan, 41
Turkey Gravy Dijon, 36
Twice-Baked Potatoes, 78
Two-Cheese Soufflé, 51

Veal Roast, Pesto-Stuffed, 23
Vegetables (*see also* **individual listings**)
    Artichoke-Stuffed Chicken Breasts, 32
    Beef Stew with Sweet Potatoes, 61
    Bountiful Bouillabaisse, 64
    Broccoli and Wild Rice Pilaf, 80
    Broccoli Bake, 74
    Caraway Turkey-Noodle Bake, 42
    Chicken Broccoli Pasta Parmesan, 29
    Creamy Chicken-Broccoli Soup, 62
    Creamy Fresh Broccoli Soup, 82
    Fresh Vegetable Marinade, 8
    Garden Vegetable Gravy, 37
    Ginger Beef Stir-Fry, 21
    Ginger-Turkey Spaghetti, 44
    Ham with Cornmeal Biscuits, 46
    Harvest Vegetables with Cheese Sauce, 71
    Herbed Fish Chowder, 63
    Herbed Tortellini Soup, 83
    Herb-Stuffed Turkey, 30
    Jalapeno Chili, 62
    Lemon Chicken Omelets, 55
    Mediterranean-Style Fettuccine, 42
    Nacho Broccoli Strata, 51
    Nacho Turkey Puff, 40
    Omelet Primavera, 52
    Piquant Pork Chops, 26
    Red and Green Stir-Fry, 72
    Sea 'n' Shore Puffy Omelet, 54
    Sierra Chicken Stew, 63
    Spicy Chicken and Vegetables, 29
    Spinach-Potato Scramble, 56
    Stuffed Mushrooms Florentine, 15
    Sweet Potato Shepherd's Pie, 41
    Sweet Potato-Stuffed Squash, 75
    Turkey-Broccoli Divan, 41
    Vegetable-Stuffed Flank Steak, 24
    Walnut Vegetable Medley, 72

Walnut Vegetable Medley, 72
White Olive Pizza, 66